" *The adventures of man's tireless mind* "
2700 B.C.   A.D. 1936

From

UR

to

ROME

by

K. M. GADD

being

HISTORY
SECONDARY SERIES
BOOK ONE

GINN AND COMPANY LTD.
QUEEN SQUARE   LONDON, W.C.1

HISTORY

SECONDARY SERIES

General Editor . . . . *Catherine B. Firth*

Note : *Each volume is accompanied by a Reference Book*

GINN AND COMPANY LTD.

7 QUEEN SQUARE   LONDON W.C. 1

124106

Printed in Great Britain by R. & R. CLARK, LIMITED, *Edinburgh.*

PREFACE

From Ur to Rome is a book of beginnings, for it seeks to show the origins of our present civilization in the remote past. The structure of European society is raised on foundations laid long ago in the valley of the Tigris and Euphrates and in the countries bordering on the Mediterranean Sea. There the first steps in material and economic progress, in social and political organization, and in spiritual awakening were taken. Without some knowledge of its beginnings our complex environment can be but imperfectly understood.

At the age of eleven it is the particular, rather than the general, that appeals, and detail is of absorbing interest. Much that would be in place in an outline of ancient history has therefore been omitted from this book ; what has been included has been treated with such detail as space allows. To perceive the familiar in an unfamiliar setting ; to find the pieces of the puzzle fitting neatly into place ; to realize that, though change is the woof, continuity is the warp in the stuff of history : these are joys which can be experienced by the child as well as by the adult. History is, above all, a humane study. It is the human interest which is placed in the forefront in this book.

The eleven-year-old is an eager and persistent questioner. In the *reference book* which accompanies this volume there are extracts from contemporary sources and historical notes which will help to answer his questions. The majority of the extracts and the simpler notes can be used by the pupils with a minimum of help from the teacher. Exercises which offer further opportunity for independent work are suggested, and lists of dates and other material useful for reference are given.

As the first of a series, this volume tries to lay the foundations on which others may build. On the success of its endeavour will depend largely the pupils' reaction to the material presented in the later volumes. Yet an author, writing for boys and girls in general, cannot hope to meet entirely the needs of individual pupils of varying attainments and rates of progress. Adaptation to individual need can only be made by the teacher, who is a partner with the author in the task to be achieved.

It is my privilege here to thank the many friends who have given me unstinted help, especially the late Sir E. A. Wallis Budge, who discussed with me the first twelve chapters, and Professor J. H. Sleeman, of the University of London, who has read the chapters on Greece and given me many valuable suggestions. I have also to thank Miss D. Avery, of the School of the Convent of Notre Dame de Sion, London, and Miss M. C. Hughes, of the Secondary School for Girls, Northampton, for their illuminating comments. I cannot hope that the book is free from mistakes ; they are fewer than they would have been but for the generous help of these and other friends.

I wish to express my gratitude to those authors, publishers, and learned societies who have given permission for the use of quotations and pictures, particulars of which will be found in the reference book ; and I would offer my special thanks to the publishers for their ever-ready help and unending patience.

KATHLEEN M. GADD

London
Easter, 1936

CONTENTS

From Ur to Rome

FROM UR TO ROME

A lady of imperial Rome

CHAPTER I

The Land of the Two Rivers

Civilization began when men made stone tools. In Sumer and Egypt they soon began to use metal. We have learned much about the Sumerians and Egyptians from excavations.

"ANYTHING can happen in the long passing of time", said a wise old Greek. Many things have happened in the thousands of years that have passed since men first appeared on the earth, from the discovery of fire to the invention of wireless. But these things have not happened by chance; they have come to pass because men and women have thought and talked, planned and worked to make life better and happier for themselves and for those who would come after them. This long effort of mankind has resulted in the world in which we live to-day. The story of it we call history.

Men began the adventure of finding out when they first learned how to kindle a flame. No one knows when this took place; it was so long ago. They took a big step forward when they made stone tools with which to till the ground and produce corn for food. At the same time they built simple one-roomed houses of reeds or slender branches, woven into matting or basket-work and supported on wooden posts or bundles of reeds lashed together. They tamed wild animals ; cows and goats to give them milk, sheep to give them wool, and dogs to help them in their hunting and to guard their houses. They made rough wooden looms on which to weave cloth, and clay pots

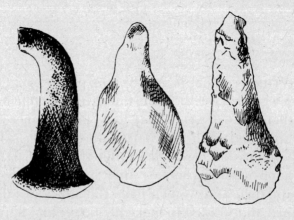

and flint knives for use in their homes. Thus they gained for themselves food, clothing, and shelter, the three necessities which people in all ages must have before they can think about other things. We to-day are just as much concerned to obtain these necessities as the men of long ago, but we do not need to think so much about them. The use of money, the invention of machinery, and the improvements in transport that have been made between their time and ours have made them much easier to get.

All over the world men began civilized life in this way. The civilization of every great nation goes back to these beginnings. The earliest known civilization came into being, about the same time, in two countries, Egypt and Mesopotamia.

Mesopotamia is the name given to the fertile valley watered by two rivers, the Tigris and the Euphrates. In very ancient times the lower part of this valley consisted of marshes and lagoons. No one could live there. So the stone-using inhabitants lived in the upper part of the valley. But, as years went by, the lagoons became dry land; for in their long journey from the mountains of Asia Minor to the Persian Gulf, the rivers brought down with them much fine soil, which gradually piled up at the head of the gulf. This soil was so rich that crops would grow in it easily; thus it attracted wandering tribes to settle in it.

To it came the Sumerians, and from them the land came to be called Sumer. They came probably from the highlands of north-western India, and brought with them the knowledge of how to work metal. This was important; first of all because there was no stone in the delta land, and secondly because people can make things far better with metal tools than with stone ones. So the Sumerians progressed quickly, building their houses of bricks which they made from the clay of the river banks, and decorating their bowls and vases with patterns done in red and black paint. They made boats of plaited reeds covered with skins and pitch, and in these they

caught fish among the marshes that still remained at the mouths of the rivers. Instead of living in villages, they gathered together in little towns, from which they made canals out into the sandy desert to water the land. Soon they had more corn and wool than was necessary for their needs, and so they exchanged them with their neighbours for the copper, timber, and stone which they lacked. This was the beginning of trade. Since that time trade has grown steadily till it has become one of the most important things in the world. Without trade we could not even get our food to-day.

When the Sumerians first settled in Mesopotamia, they were without many things familiar to us. They had no method of writing except by drawing pictures on lumps of clay. Even when they had turned their

pictures into signs and begun to write, they used their
newly discovered art chiefly for business affairs. They

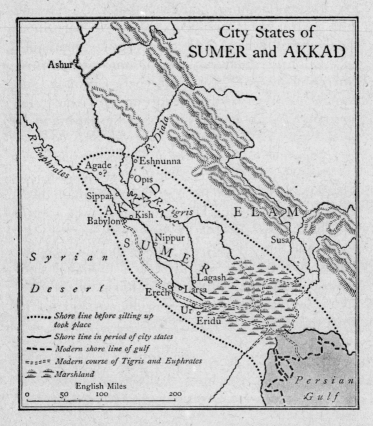

did not write about their own lives. We have found
out how they lived in another way. In many places
in Mesopotamia are long low mounds under which
are buried the ancient cities of the Sumerians. About

eighty years ago, people who were interested in the
distant past began to dig in these mounds, and they
found there remains of houses and palaces, tombs and
temples, from which we have been able to learn about
the lives and ideas of the people. To-day many such
excavations are being carried on, some by the British
Government, others by the French, Germans, and
Americans. As a result, scholars are now able to tell
us something about the history of the land and its
people.

Under one of the mounds in Sumer lies the city of
Ur, the place from which Abraham set out with his
family to the land of Canaan. When Abraham dwelt
there nearly four thousand years ago, it was already
ancient; almost as old as its neighbour, Eridu,
which, the Sumerians said, was the first of all cities.
The story of Ur, as revealed by excavation, will show
us what Sumerian civilization was like, for throughout the land people lived in the same way and did the
same things.

CHAPTER II

Ur of the Chaldees

The Sumerians lived in cities. They built their houses and temples of brick. They made canals to carry water into the desert around their cities. They traded with other countries.

THE city of Abraham was built on the bank of the Euphrates. It was surrounded by a high brick wall and a broad canal, which formed a waterway as well as a means of defence, if this were necessary. On the river frontage was a large harbour, in which boats bringing merchandise by way of the Euphrates could be moored. There was another harbour in the northern part of the city, which was connected with the river by a canal running through the city. These harbours and canals show how much the trade of the city had increased since it was first founded.

Within the walls ran a number of narrow winding streets, such as can be seen in many old towns to-day. But they were not tarred or paved as our streets are ; they were simply lanes of trodden earth, baked hard by the sun. Lining these streets were houses and shops. The shops were tiny places, even smaller than the little country shops of to-day. Opening on the

street was a showroom, in which the owner displayed
his goods ; behind was a storeroom, and one or two
living-rooms. There were no shop windows, for the
art of glass-making had not yet been discovered.
Houses differed in size, just as they do to-day. The
house of a rich merchant had two storeys and many

The remains of a house in Ur

rooms, while the homes of people like the water-
carriers and the porters who worked on the quays
had only a few rooms all on one floor.

One difference between a Sumerian house and a
modern house that would strike us at once is that
there were no windows opening on the street. The
Sumerians did not think fresh air and light as necessary as we do, and besides this, the sun in Eastern

lands is so hot that people want to keep it out of their houses. The brick walls on either side of the street were broken only by high narrow archways, closed by a wooden door or a reed mat. Another thing we should miss in Ur would be gardens. The only open space in a Sumerian house was a paved courtyard, round which the rooms were built. A staircase in the corner led to the second floor, where the rooms opened on to a wooden gallery, supported on pillars at each corner of the courtyard.

But though a Sumerian house was differently planned from a modern house, it was similar in many ways. There were rooms for different purposes such as we have, a room to receive visitors, storerooms and servants' rooms, a kitchen with a cooking-hearth, even, in the bigger houses, a bathroom. Many houses had also a chapel, where the family went daily to ask the blessing of the gods who looked after the household. On the second floor were the bedrooms and the family sitting-room. The walls were plastered, reed mats covered the hard clay floors, and the furniture consisted of reed stools and little tables, beds with wooden frames and reed mattresses, jugs and drinking-cups, bowls and cooking utensils of metal or pottery. Everything was simple, but in a Sumerian house we should find we could live quite comfortably. We should not have the conveniences we are used to in our own houses, but all the necessary things would be there.

A large area in the middle of the city was occupied by a walled enclosure. Within this lay a great temple. The Sumerians, of course, lived long before Christ was born, long even before the Hebrews knew that there is only one god, whom they called Yahweh

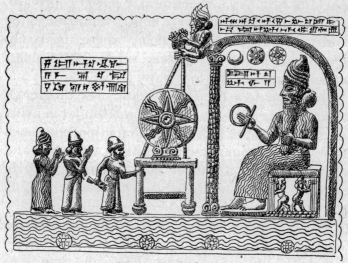

The worship of Shamash

(Jehovah). But this does not mean that they had no religion, for even in the earliest times people thought that there were powers, stronger than themselves, which must be worshipped and revered. The Sumerians believed that these powers were the forces of Nature, such as the sky, the earth, the water, the sun and moon. Each was a god with a name. The sky-god was called Anu; the others were Enlil,

Ea, Shamash, Nannar. Each god dwelt in a special city. Anu dwelt in Uruk ; Ea had his home in Eridu, near the sea ; Enlil lived in Nippur. Shamash was worshipped specially by the people of Larsa, Nannar by the people of Ur. But though the Sumerians believed that the gods were great and powerful, giving them good things if they pleased them and punishing them if they displeased them, they thought of them in the form of human beings, needing food and drink, sleep and clothing, goods and services. So, beside their houses within the city, the gods had lands outside the walls, slaves to till the soil, millers, bakers and brewers to make their bread and beer, and weavers to make their clothes.

The great temple of Nannar, which we may liken to a cathedral, stood on a terrace inside the walled enclosure. It consisted of three solid brick platforms, one on top of the other, and each smaller than the one below it. On the top platform was the little shrine in which was the image of Nannar. The second platform was reached by a triple staircase, made, like the rest of the temple, of large greyish bricks, stamped with the name of Ur-Nammu, the king who built the temple. A single staircase led to the top platform.

Around the temple-tower were the houses of the priests, just as in a cathedral city the houses of the clergy are built round the close. On the terrace were also the kitchens where Nannar's daily food was prepared. Below the terrace was a large courtyard, surrounded by storerooms, in which were kept the produce of his lands and the offerings that the people made to him.

The temple-tower was not the only place where Nannar was worshipped ; he had many smaller temples where daily services were said, just as in a cathedral town there are other churches. There were

Gathering dates

also temples for Ningal, his wife, for every god had a wife. The bigger temples were all within the enclosure, but outside it, in the streets of the city, were chapels to which people went in the course of their daily work to pray and make an offering. These were simple buildings, consisting of a paved courtyard and a little room, the sanctuary, in which was an altar and the image of the god or goddess to whom the chapel was dedicated. This was not always Nannar or Ningal, for though one god always held the chief place in a city, other gods and goddesses might be worshipped there as well.

The king's palace was also inside the temple enclosure. It was built on the same plan as an ordinary house, but it was larger, and there were many more storerooms and servants' quarters, as well as offices for his ministers and their clerks.

Beyond the walls of Ur lay cornfields and pastures, groves of date palms and onion beds. There, too, were the homes of the farmers and the labourers who tilled the ground. Some were perched on little knolls or artificial mounds among the fields, to be out of reach of the spring floods, others were clustered under the walls of the city. The farmhouses were built of brick ; the houses of the labourers were more often one-roomed structures of reeds, like those of the stone-using people of earlier times. Byres, granaries, and sheep-pens were also built in this simple fashion.

This was the city of Ur, as it appeared about 2000 B.C. A traveller, going up the Euphrates, would pass many similar cities, each surrounded by cornfields and canals, and inhabited by a thriving population.

CHAPTER III

The dwellers in a Sumerian city

In Sumer the priests were the learned men. Each city was ruled by a king. Merchants and craftsmen lived in the cities. Farmers grew corn outside the city walls. There were many slaves.

IN a Sumerian town the classes of people were much the same as in a modern town, though they differed in numbers and importance. The priests were the most important people, for they were the servants of the god who protected the city, caused the corn to grow, and gave health and happiness to everybody. They had much work to do besides conducting the services in the temples and offering the sacrifices. They looked after the temple lands which lay outside the city : they saw that the produce was stored in the god's warehouses and kept careful accounts of everything that came into and went out of them. They carried on trade for the god, exchanging his surplus corn, wool, dates, and skins for the stone and timber, the gold, silver, and incense that were needed for his temples. They supervised the servants who cooked the food and made the beer that were placed every day before the image of the god in every temple.

With all this work to do, it is not surprising that in every Sumerian town a large number of people belonged to the priesthood. Beside men, there were women also among the priesthood, for the singing and dancing in the great processions on festival days were led by priestesses. Some of the services of the god were also performed by them. Many of them were high-born ladies, and the chief priestess was often the king's daughter.

As the priests were the only highly educated people among the Sumerians, they were also teachers, doctors, judges, and astronomers. They kept schools in the temple enclosure. They sat in the gate of the temple to settle disputes among the people and to punish those who had sinned against the gods. They spent much of their time observing the moon and the stars, for the Sumerians believed that these had a great deal to do with the conduct of their lives. If a man were going to set out on a journey, he would go to the priests to find out when a star which would bring him good fortune would be in the sky. The priests also found a meaning in the position of the stars : " If the Yoke-star rises with its face towards the west and looks at the face of heaven, and no wind blows at all, there will be famine. . . ."

The priests also kept the calendar, reckoning each month by the rising and setting of the moon. They had twelve months in every year as we have, divided into days and hours. But each month had only thirty

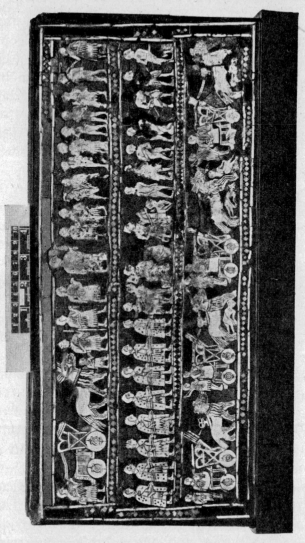

A Sumerian king goes to war

days, making a year of three hundred and sixty days instead of three hundred and sixty-five, which is the length of the year according to the movement of the sun. So in order to keep the winter months in the dark cold part of the year and the summer months in the sunny warm time, an extra month was added when the priests said it was necessary.

The people went to the priests for healing, because they believed that illness was due to the anger of the gods. In the ruins of temples excavators have found many clay tablets, on which doctors' prescriptions are written. Some of them contain curious things that we should think would make us worse instead of better, but some of the herbs put into medicines and ointments are still in use. Medicine, however, was not the most important thing in curing an illness ; it was far more important that the doctor should say certain words over the patient. For a toothache, which was thought to be due to a worm in the tooth, he would say : "O Worm, may Ea smite thee with the might of his fist". Only the priests knew exactly what should be said for different illnesses.

Equal in importance to the priests was the king. In very early days the Sumerians had no kings. The chief priest ruled the city. But as the cities grew in size, the work of government became too much for the chief priest. So, just as many centuries later, among the Hebrews, Samuel anointed Saul, the chief priest chose a man from among the priesthood to rule the people. This was the beginning of kingship, a form of government which still exists in many countries.

A king in Sumer had, however, many more duties to perform than the king has to-day. At the great festivals he offered the sacrifices to the god. He managed all the affairs of the city which were not connected with the temple worship. He kept order among the people, built and repaired the city walls, and made canals and harbours. He led the army in battle. This occupied a good deal of his time, for the Sumerian cities were constantly quarrelling with one another. Often the quarrel began over the ownership of land near two neighbouring cities. To settle the matter the cities went to war, for there was then no League of Nations. The stronger city, having defeated the weaker one, took it under its rule. The king of a strong city often ruled over many other cities, and then he was called " the mighty man, the king of the four regions ", that is, the lands north, south, east, and west of the city. A city might keep the kingship of the land for two or three hundred years, but then other stronger rulers would arise and take the kingship in their turn. In this way, the chief city in the land was constantly changing; sometimes it was Ur, at other times Erech or Lagash or Nippur.

The king was helped in the task of government by ministers and servants, who were among the richest and most important people in the city. Some were judges, for the king shared with the priests the work of doing justice and seeing that the laws were kept. Many were occupied in carrying out the king's commands, both in his own city and in other cities under his rule. Others saw that the goods which were given to him by the people, the equivalent of the taxes we pay, were duly sent and stored in his treasury. Others were employed in looking after his household and his lands, and in carrying on trade for him. This trade was very extensive, for the king lived in great state ; he needed gold and silver and jewels in great quantities for all the beautiful things he had in his

A king's gold drinking-vessel

palace, for the adornment of his wife and her ladies, and for the decoration of the temple of his god.

The priests and the king's officials formed the upper classes. Next to them came the middle classes, which included merchants, skilled craftsmen, and farmers. The merchants were the wealthier citizens, who carried on business with other cities and other countries. In their warehouses on the quays they stored the produce of the city's lands, the surplus that remained when the farmers had provided for their own needs, paid their taxes to the king, and made their offerings to the gods. Wheat and barley, dates and wool were carefully weighed with big stone weights, and done up in bales with the cord secured by lumps of clay, stamped with the merchant's seal. Then they were carried to their destination by his employees. Sometimes they were transported by donkey caravans across the desert, sometimes by boats on the Euphrates, or, a longer and more dangerous journey, by sea. In exchange the traders brought back the raw materials needed by the craftsmen; cedar wood from Lebanon, stone from the mountains to the north of the valley, copper and silver from the Taurus Mountains. Carnelian and lapis-lazuli came from Elam, ivory from Africa, and gold from Asia Minor and India. All these precious goods then passed into the hands of the craftsmen; stone to the builders for door sockets and to the sculptors for carving and statuary; timber to the wood-workers for doors and gates; copper to the armourers for weapons and to the metal-workers for bowls and drinking-cups; gold, silver, and precious stones to the goldsmiths. Craftsmen who did work of this kind were among the better-class citizens; other craftsmen, who made articles like pottery, leather goods, and reed furniture, were not so well off, for their goods were less valuable. The farmers who lived outside the city, if they were free men, also belonged to the middle classes, which, as in modern times, included people of varying degrees of wealth and position.

Slaves formed the lowest class in Sumerian society. They were the servants in the households of the richer people ; they worked on the land, and in the workshops of the craftsmen (some of them were even small craftsmen themselves), and did all the

A farmer ploughing and sowing

harder labour in the city, such as street-cleaning, water-carrying, and porterage. But though they were slaves, they were not usually harshly treated ; for the Sumerians were not cruel to their slaves, provided they behaved well. Many of them had homes and property of their own ; and often, if they could save enough to pay for it, they were given their freedom. It was only if they tried to run away that they were severely punished.

Only a few of the children in a Sumerian city went to school ; the others helped in the work of the household or the business. Girls helped their mothers with the baking and the brewing, the cooking and the weaving ; boys helped on the farm or in the workshop. But they had some time for play. Excavators have found their playthings, clay or wooden dolls, and waggons and animals on wheels. They had some holidays, for the festivals of the gods were holidays for everybody. Then they went with their parents to watch the procession and to join in the general feasting and rejoicing, as the image of the god was carried through the streets of the city or rowed in his sacred barge along the canals to bless the fields.

CHAPTER IV

Artists and craftsmen in Sumer

Sumertan craftsmen made gold and silver vessels, and weapons and tools of copper. Artists made stone statues and pictures with pieces of stone and shell. The seal-cutters were busy people.

MANY things made by artists and craftsmen have been found in the mound of Ur. Some of these were discovered among the ruins of buildings, and others in graves which were probably those of the early kings and queens of Ur. It seems curious that bowls and drinking-vessels, helmets and jewellery, harps and chariots should be found in graves. But the Sumerians believed that, in the world to which they went after death, they would need all the things they had had when alive. So their relations buried such things with them.

The graves in which some of the finest work has been found are more than five thousand years old. In those days there were no machines or tools worked by electricity, such as the modern craftsman has to

I   23   C

aid him in doing fine work. Everything was done by hand with a few simple copper tools, and yet the Sumerian workmen produced most beautiful things. Many of them can be seen to-day in the British Museum. Finely shaped bowls of creamy alabaster were ground out until the light shone clearly through them, and polished with sand until they were as smooth as velvet to the touch. Golden drinking-vessels were delicately fluted, and plain polished bowls were engraved with the name of the owner. Weapons and armour were also placed in the graves. A prince called Meskalam-Shar had a wonderful golden helmet, shaped like a wig. Every wave and curl of the hair was shown, and the long ends behind were done up in a little knot just like a woman's hair to-day. Queens and princesses had their jewellery; large gold earrings, head-dresses of golden ribbon adorned with tiny leaves and pomegranates, necklaces and bracelets of carnelian and lapis-lazuli, and pins for fastening their dresses with heads in the shape of animals.

Besides articles of dress, weapons, and vessels for food and drink, these kings and queens had harps of silver adorned with bulls' heads in gold and lapis-lazuli, gaming-boards inlaid with patterns of coloured shell (as modern workmen inlay furniture with ebony and ivory), wooden sledges inlaid with shell designs, and chariots of wood covered with skin. All these things show us how wonderfully skilled were

the Sumerian craftsmen in these very early times, and how rich were the kings who could afford to buy all the gold and silver and precious stones found in their tombs.

Among the most skilled craftsmen in Sumer were the seal-cutters. All the important people in a Sumerian city had a seal. Kings, priests, and ministers needed them for their letters, and merchants for their business. These seals were small cylinders of clay or stone, or even expensive materials like alabaster, ivory, and lapis-lazuli. They were carved all round with pictures of gods, animals, or human beings, and there was a hole through the middle to which a small handle could be attached. When the seal was used, it was rolled across the clay tablet, on which the letter was written, while it was still damp, and thus the impression of the picture was left on the clay. We use a similar device to-day with our signet rings and sealing-wax.

Sumerian sculptors made statues for the temples of the gods. These were often figures of priests with completely bald heads, for it was the custom of the priests to shave their heads as well as their chins. Sometimes they made statues of the gods also. In one temple excavators have found the figure of Ab-u, the lord of growing things : he has long wavy hair and a beard, and is dressed in a plain woollen skirt, ornamented at the bottom with a fringe. With him is his wife, who wears the ordinary dress of Sumerian women, a long piece of woollen cloth wrapped round her body, passing under her right arm and over her left shoulder, where it was fastened with a large pin.

The skill of the Sumerian artists is shown also by the decorations of the temple of the goddess Nin-khursag, which stood four miles from Ur. It was built by King A-anni-padda, who reigned about 2900 B.C. It stood on a platform and was approached by a wide brick stairway. The doorway had columns on either side, made of trunks of palm trees, which were coated with pitch and covered with triangular pieces of mother-of-pearl and red and black stone, to form a mosaic. Above the doorway was a wooden panel, carved with a lion-headed eagle, holding two stags in its claws. The whole carving was covered with thin copper plates, fastened to the wood with little copper nails. On either side of the door was a lion's head, made in a similar way, with coloured eyes and red protruding tongues. These fierce-looking animals were to guard the temple against the evil spirits who were always seeking to enter it.

Many other statues and carvings adorned the front of the temple. Standing or lying at the foot of the walls were rows of copper bulls, with beautifully modelled heads and horns. On the walls themselves were bands of decoration, a procession of bulls and another of ducks, and a frieze showing the cows of Nin-khursag being milked by the temple herdsmen, while other servants made the milk into butter. All these friezes were made by setting figures, cut out in stone or shell, into a background of pitch, and bordering each band with copper.

Though there were clever sculptors in Sumer, there were no painters of pictures. What pictures the Sumerians possessed were made in somewhat the same way as a mosaic is made to-day. Figures were cut out in red and white shell, and stuck in a thin layer of pitch spread on a wooden panel. The background was filled in with lapis-lazuli, and the whole picture was framed in a border of red and white shell. Two pictures of this kind have been found in a prince's grave. One is a scene of warfare. The king, dressed only in a sheepskin skirt, receives naked prisoners of war. Foot soldiers are marching in a column, each with his leather helmet, his stout copper-tipped spear, and his woollen cloak, which he threw off when going into action. Besides the foot soldiers, there is a line of chariots, light vehicles made of wood and leather, drawn by four asses. Each chariot is just large enough to hold the driver, and on the step behind stands a spearman. The picture shows these men in the act of hurling their spears at the enemy soldiers, who are falling dead and wounded beneath the feet of the galloping animals.

Another way of making a picture was to carve it on a stone slab. A picture of this kind was set up in the temple at Ur by order of King Ur-Nammu, who reigned about 2250 B.C. Ur-Nammu was a great builder. He made many canals around the city. One of his inscriptions says, " For Nannar, his king, Ur-Nammu, the mighty man, king of Ur, king of Sumer and Akkad, has dug the great canal, his beloved canal ". He also rebuilt the city wall and the temple-tower of Nannar. His carved picture showed scenes in the building of the temple, such as the god Nannar giving him a rod, a ring, and a measuring-line, the chief tools needed by an architect. This picture, besides showing the skill of the Sumerian artist, tells us many things about the ways of the people. Nannar is seated on a reed stool, such as people used in their houses ; he wears a flounced dress and a high crown. The king, who wears a long woollen robe and a close-fitting cap, is pouring out before him a libation or drink-offering from a vessel shaped exactly like those found in the graves of the kings of nearly a thousand years earlier.

Most of the things which tell us of the arts and crafts of the Sumerians have been found at Ur, for this is the place which has been most fully excavated. But excavations in other parts of Mesopotamia have revealed things of a similar nature, which show that Ur was not exceptional in the wealth of its kings and the skill of its workers. Each ruler, as he became in his turn rich and powerful, sought to beautify his city, as well as the other cities which came under his rule. This gave employment to people and increased trade, so that under a strong king the land prospered.

CHAPTER V

Sargon and Hammurabi

Sargon, king of Akkad, ruled a wide empire. Hammurabi of Babylon was the first lawgiver.

To the north of Sumer lay the land of Akkad. No mountain barriers separated it from Sumer. So the people moved easily between the two lands, and in early days Akkad was inhabited by Sumerians. But at some time about which we know very little, another people came into the land. They were Semites, of the same race as the Hebrews, who settled in Palestine more than a thousand years later. Though good soldiers, the Semites were not as civilized as the Sumerians. They had no writing of their own, and no skilled craftsmen. So the Akkadian rulers encouraged their people to learn from the Sumerians. Their scribes were taught to write the Semitic language with Sumerian signs. They built houses for themselves in Sumerian fashion and temple-towers for their gods, many of whom were given Sumerian names.

At a little place called Eshnunna, the remains of an Akkadian temple and an Akkadian palace have been found. The temple had a vaulted roof, which only skilled builders could make in brick. The palace had many rooms and courtyards, and beside it ran a big brick-built sewer, with which were connected smaller drains from the palace. Among the ruins were found finely cut cylinder seals, beautiful jewellery of silver, lapis-lazuli and carnelian, copper bowls, lamps and knives. All these show how the Akkadians had learnt craftsmanship from the Sumerians, and how the Akkadian kings, like the Sumerian rulers, traded with far-off lands.

The probable appearance of the temple of Ab-u, the god of vegetation

The Akkadians dwelt in cities, like the Sumerians, and some of their rulers were powerful kings. Sometimes, indeed, they ruled over the land of Sumer as well. The greatest of these Akkadian kings, who was called Sargon, lived about 2500 B.C.

There is a story which tells how Sargon's mother, being too poor to keep him, put him in a basket of reeds and cast him into the river. He was rescued by a poor man called Akki, who brought him up to be a gardener like himself. From being a gardener, Sargon became a servant of the king of Kish. Then, with the help of the goddess Ishtar, he raised himself to the position of cupbearer to the king. Finally he became king himself, choosing the city of Agade for his chief city.

Sargon was a fine soldier. Gradually he conquered all the cities of Akkad and then of Sumer. Erech, Nippur, Lagash, Umma, Ur, and Eridu all became subject to him, and his ships of war sailed the Persian Gulf, fighting against the Elamites. Then he turned northwards, and after many years of warfare he extended his power to the coasts of Phoenicia and the Mediterranean Sea. Thus he ruled the land " from the Lower to the Upper Sea ", and created the first empire in history.

Another great king whose city was in the land of Akkad was Hammurabi, who reigned six hundred years after Sargon. He, too, was a Semite; but, like Sargon, he used the Sumerian writing and encouraged his people to follow the Sumerian manners and customs. His city of Babylon, which formerly had been only a small place, became a fine walled city,

in which was the temple of Marduk, the special god
of the Babylonians. The gods of the Sumerians were
also worshipped by the Babylonians, whose priests
learned all the lore of the Sumerian priests ; the
magic words with which to cure illnesses, the knowledge of the stars, and the old Sumerian stories of the
Creation and the Flood, and of the hero Gilgamesh.

The Babylonians tilled the land and
made canals like the Sumerians ; they
traded in the same way, and used their
weights and measures and their way
of reckoning time. So that life in the
city of Babylon was much the same as
that in a Sumerian city. The chief
difference was that the people spoke a
different tongue, since they belonged
to a different race.

*An Akkadian
lady*

Hammurabi, like Sargon, ruled over
wide lands, defended by his well-trained
army. He looked after all the cities
subject to him carefully. He tells us himself how
he adorned the temple of Marduk at Nippur and
cleansed the temple of Ea at Eridu, how he enlarged
the palace at Kish, built granaries at Dilbat, and
furnished water to the people of Erech by building
a great canal. Some people think that it was in
Hammurabi's time that Abraham lived at Ur.

Many of the letters which Hammurabi sent by his
special postmen to the governors of different cities

are to-day in the British Museum. Some of them are about trade, for the king wished that his country should be rich as well as powerful. If any merchant found that he was hindered in his trade by any means, he had only to make a complaint to the king, and his case would be enquired into. Other letters give orders that the canals shall be properly kept, for the king watched as carefully over the crops and the cattle of the land as he did over its trade.

Hammurabi has been called the first lawgiver. Before his time each city in Sumer and Akkad had its own laws. Clay tablets on which some of them were written have been found in the temples, but they were for the use of the priests only, when they judged the people. Hammurabi wished the people also to know the laws. He collected the old laws and added some new ones. Then he had them engraved by skilful stone-cutters on a great block of black stone, and set up in front of a statue of himself in the temple of Marduk, where all the people could see them. At the top of the stone was a picture of Shamash, who was the supreme judge of gods and men as well as the sun-god, giving the laws to Hammurabi, just as, in the Bible story, Yahweh gave the Ten Command-ments to Moses. Underneath the picture were written the two hundred and eighty-two laws that Hammurabi wished the people to obey. At the end of his code the king says, " In the future, in days to come, let the king who is in the land guard the words

" The judgments of righteousness, which Hammurabi, the great king, set up "

of righteousness I have written on my *stelê*. Let him not alter the judgment of the land which I judged, nor the decisions I decided."

Some of Hammurabi's laws seem very harsh. A man who built a house for another so carelessly that it fell down and killed the owner was to be put to death. If a man fought with another and knocked out one of his teeth, then his own tooth was to be knocked out. People who neglected to cultivate their land or did not keep the canal in proper order had to pay heavy fines in silver or in goods. Other laws were meant to help the poor. Doctors were not allowed to charge poor people as much as they charged the rich, and the charges of boatmen on the river and other people doing public service were carefully laid down.

Even if Hammurabi's laws were severe, they were good because he tried to be just to everybody. Indeed they were so good that gradually they became used in lands outside Babylonia. In the Book of Exodus there are laws which are very like those of Hammurabi. Some of the laws in the Old Testament were given to the Hebrews by Moses ; but the others were drawn up by Jewish lawgivers many years later, and scholars think the men who drew them up used the laws of Hammurabi as their guide. Thus it is in Babylonia, nearly four thousand years ago, that we find the beginnings of the habit of obedience to written law which makes our lives so secure to-day.

CHAPTER VI

The land of the Pharaohs

The Egyptians prayed to the Nile. The Pharaohs ruled Egypt.

THE Egyptian schoolboy repeats, " Egypt is the Nile and the Nile is Egypt ". Two thousand five hundred years ago Herodotus, a Greek historian, said much the same thing. Without the yearly Nile flood, there would be no Egypt ; for the country is almost rainless, and the river valley is barren and stony, like the desert that rolls away above the white limestone cliffs on either side of it. The Egyptian prays, not for a good harvest, but for a good Nile. In ancient days, when men understood less about the natural causes of the rise of the river, they regarded it as a god, offered prayers and sacrifices to it, and sang hymns in praise of it :

> Blessed be the good God,
> The heaven-loving Nile,
>
> .   .   .   .
>
> The plenty, wealth, and food of Egypt.
> He maketh everybody live by himself.
> Riches are in his path,
> And plenteousness is in his fingers.

The Nile rises in the highlands of Central Africa, and winds its way through a narrow valley to the Mediterranean Sea. Near the coast, where the hills cease, the river divides into many channels, forming a delta of low-lying land. When the snow melts on the mountains at the river's source, the flood brings down with it quantities of fine black earth. When the waters subside, this earth is left as a layer of fertile soil, stretching away on either side of the river as far as the flood water has extended. To the ancient Egyptian the rise of the flood meant life or death. If it rose well, there would be plenteous crops and green pastures for the cattle; if it failed to rise, there would be starvation for man and beast. The Bible story of Pharaoh's dream, with Joseph's interpretation of it, is a story of the Nile. The seven fat kine are the years of plenty when there was a good Nile; the seven lean kine mean the famine which followed a low Nile.

The early Egyptians called the valley in which they lived the Black Land; the desert above the cliffs, the home of lions, wolves, hyenas, and jackals, was the Red Land. Like the earliest people in Mesopotamia, they lived a simple life, dwelling in mud and reed huts, using stone tools for tilling the land, and flint for their knives, arrow-heads, and spear-points. Probably they had already discovered copper, but they did not use it much because it was so rare.

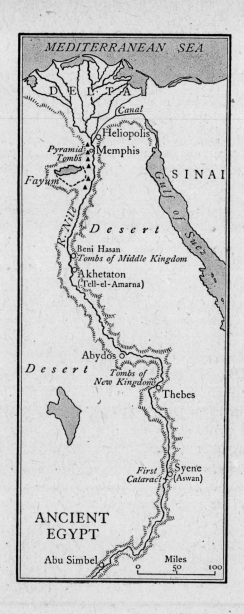

MEDITERRANEAN SEA

DELTA

Canal

Heliopolis

Pyramid
Tombs

Memphis

Fayum

SINAI

Gulf of Suez

Desert

Beni Hasan
Tombs of Middle Kingdom

Akhetaton
(Tell-el-Amarna)

R. Nile

Abydos

Desert

Tombs of
New Kingdom

Thebes

First
Cataract

Syene
(Aswan)

ANCIENT
EGYPT

Abu Simbel

Miles

0   50   100

The Egyptians learned to write about the same time as the Sumerians, that is, more than five thousand years ago. Like the Sumerians, they wrote at first with pictures. But they kept their picture writing, which we call hieroglyphic, far longer than the Sumerians. The priests used it for thousands of years. It is from hieroglyphic inscriptions, which

Early Egyptians

were often written on the walls of tombs and temples, that we have learned most of what we know about the ancient Egyptians.

Among other things, these inscriptions tell us that about 3000 B.C. the land of Egypt was ruled by a king, who was called Pharaoh, from the Egyptian word for the great house in which he lived. His capital was Memphis, a city at the head of the Nile delta. To help him in the task of governing, he had many officials and servants, some of whom lived in and around his palace and formed his court, while others went out into distant parts of the kingdom to see that his commands were carried out. For many hundreds of years kings ruled the land in this way. Then the nobles and royal servants gained land for themselves, set up big households of their own, and taught the people to obey them instead of the king. At last there was no longer one king in the land, but several kings, all fighting against one another and destroying the peace and prosperity of the people.

This went on for over two hundred years. Then about 2100 B.C. a noble, greater than the rest, made himself king of the whole land once more. This kingdom is called the Middle Kingdom, to distinguish it from the earlier one, the Old Kingdom. The new king set up his capital at Thebes, higher up the Nile than Memphis. For a time there was peace and order in Egypt, and the Pharaohs began to conquer other lands, sending their armies into Nubia, a country rich in gold, and across the sea to the coasts of Palestine. Then the nobles rebelled again, and foreigners from Asia came pouring into the land. These invaders were stronger and more warlike than the Egyptians, who were by nature a peace-loving people. They had war-chariots and swift horses, which were then unknown in Egypt, so they were better equipped for fighting. They conquered the land and ruled it for many years. But the Egyptians hated their foreign rulers, and at last a leader arose in Thebes who drove out the invaders and founded the

New Kingdom of Egypt, with himself as Pharaoh.

The New Kingdom, which began in 1580 B.C., is sometimes called the Empire; for the Pharaohs of this time not only restored order in their kingdom, but also extended their rule far beyond the boundaries of Egypt. They reconquered Nubia, which had been

Bringing tribute to Pharaoh

lost by the foreign kings, and through its riches they added greatly to their wealth and power. Egyptian armies crossed the desert of Sinai, and made war on the tribes of Palestine and Syria, the Canaanites and Amorites of the Bible. One of the greatest of the conquering Pharaohs, Thutmose III, attacked and took Kadesh, the chief Syrian stronghold. The tribal warriors were no match for the Egyptian soldiery, who, though they only wore the linen kilt which was the usual dress of the Egyptians, had their heads protected with quilted leather caps and carried shields, bronze spears and battle-axes. Nor could they withstand the skilful archers and the swift horse-chariots which the Pharaohs now used. So Thutmose carried on his conquering campaigns, until he had overrun all Syria and reached the river Euphrates.

This great empire almost disappeared in the time of a later Pharaoh, Akhnaton, who was not a warlike king. He was far more interested in building his beautiful city of Akhetaton, where he worshipped the god Aton, whom he thought to be the one true god, instead of the many gods of Egypt. He took no notice of the letters which his governors in Syria sent him telling him how the people were rebelling and how tribes from the desert, the Hebrews, were invading the land. When he died, Syria was lost to Egypt; but a little later two soldier Pharaohs, Seti I and Ramses II, restored the Egyptian Empire. Ramses had to fight another enemy, the Hittites, who lived to the north of Syria. Once again Kadesh was the scene of a great battle. The Hittites were far better soldiers than the Syrian tribes. Ramses says, in a long account which he wrote of the battle, that it was a great victory for him, but in reality he was very nearly beaten, and was obliged to make a treaty with the Hittite king. In spite of this, the Egyptian Empire was the greatest kingdom of the East at this time, and so it remained until the rise of the great empire of Assyria.

CHAPTER VII

Pyramids and temples

The Pharaohs were buried under pyramids. Their bodies were mummified. The Egyptians worshipped many gods in stone temples. They adorned their temples with carved and painted pictures.

THE Egyptian Pharaohs were not always fighting. Some of them hardly went to war at all, and even warrior Pharaohs were able also to govern the kingdom well and to do much good for their people. Like the Sumerian and Babylonian kings, they made canals to irrigate the land, after the flood had subsided. They were great builders of temples for the gods and of massive tombs for themselves. Herodotus, who travelled in Egypt in the fifth century B.C., tells us of the buildings of the Egyptian kings. Many of these are still to be seen. Every visitor to Egypt goes to see the pyramids which stand beneath the western cliffs of the Nile valley, not far from the modern city of Cairo.

These pyramids were the tombs of three Pharaohs of the Old Kingdom, Khufu, Khafra, and Menkaura. They are piles of solid stone masonry, four-sided and square at the base, with sides sloping upwards to a

Pharaoh Khafra

point at the top. Underneath this mass of stonework is the chamber, hollowed out in the rock, in which the body of the Pharaoh was laid. It was reached by a passage leading down from an opening in the side of the pyramid, filled in after the body was laid in the tomb chamber. Each pyramid had a temple built against one side of it, and a covered causeway led down from this to another temple, built at the point to which the flood usually rose. These temples have now almost disappeared, for the stones have been carried away to make new buildings, but the great pyramids still remain.

The building of these tombs required a great deal of labour. The stone had to be quarried and dressed by the Pharaoh's quarrymen in the rocky deserts between the Nile and the Red Sea. Then, in the flood season, gangs of labourers, who could not work on the land while it was under water, dragged the large blocks on wooden sledges to the edge of the flood. Here they loaded them on rafts by means of wooden levers, and floated them across the valley to the western edge of the flood. More labourers then dragged them to the place where the masons were at work with their measuring-lines, skilfully fitting each block into its place to give the right shape to the pyramid. As the building progressed, sloping banks of earth and sun-dried bricks were made to haul the stones up to the level of the builders. For all this work enormous numbers of men were required. Herodotus says that, according to stories he had heard, it took twenty years to build Khufu's pyramid, with one hundred thousand men working on it for three months in every year. Around the Pharaoh's pyramid were smaller ones, marking the burial places of his wife and daughters. The great nobles of the court also had their tombs built around the pyramids, so that they might still be near their master when they were dead. These were oblong stone chambers, not pyramids. Only the members of the royal family had pyramid tombs.

People have often asked why the Pharaohs spent so much time and labour on their tombs. The answer to this question is to be found in the Egyptian belief about what happened to people after death. They thought, as we do, that a man's spirit lived on, but they could not think of a spirit apart from a body. They thought that the spirit still needed the body, and so they took every care to preserve it. It was kept from decay by treating it with natron, a kind of salt, and with various spices ; then it was wrapped in yards of linen bandages. The mummy, as a body treated in this way is called, was put in a wooden coffin, often beautifully painted. This was enclosed in a stone coffin and placed in the tomb chamber, which was firmly secured so that no harm could befall the body and make it unfit for the spirit's use.

In the tomb were also placed all the things that a man had needed when he was alive. Poor people had jars and bowls with food and drink in their graves ; rich people also had clothing, weapons, jewellery, models of boats and houses and servants. The richer a man was, the more things he had in his burial chamber. As the Pharaoh was the first person in the land, his tomb was bigger and better furnished than anybody else's, and more care was taken to protect his body from harm.

The pyramid temples were for the religious services which were necessary for the soul of the dead king. They were looked after by priests, who offered prayers for the dead man and saw that the daily supplies of food and drink were prepared. The remains of Khafra's valley temple are still to be seen. Its limestone walls were lined with red granite, brought from distant Syene. Its roof was supported by square columns, each consisting of a single piece of highly polished granite. Beside each column was a statue of King Khafra, carved out of hard black stone, called diorite. One of these can be seen to-day in the Cairo Museum. Another wonderful piece of sculpture still exists close to Khafra's pyramid. It is known to us as the Sphinx. It is a mighty figure carved out of the solid rock, with the body of a lion and the head of a man. So big is this monument that a number of men can stand on one of its paws, and between the two there is sufficient space for a small temple.

The nobles also had their tomb temples within the stone chambers which covered their burial places. In them were placed their statues, showing them as they had been in life, even to the colouring of their hair and eyes. The walls were covered with carved and painted pictures of the things with which they had been surrounded during their lifetime, for the Egyptians thought that, if the actual things or the models of them were lacking, a picture would do instead. It is from these wall pictures that we have learned much of what we know about the daily life of the Egyptians.

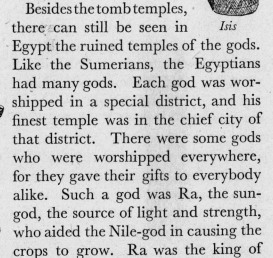

Isis

Ra

Besides the tomb temples, there can still be seen in Egypt the ruined temples of the gods. Like the Sumerians, the Egyptians had many gods. Each god was worshipped in a special district, and his finest temple was in the chief city of that district. There were some gods who were worshipped everywhere, for they gave their gifts to everybody alike. Such a god was Ra, the sun-god, the source of light and strength, who aided the Nile-god in causing the crops to grow. Ra was the king of heaven, and the Pharaoh, the strong and beneficent earthly king, was said to be his son.

Other gods generally worshipped were Osiris and Isis, and their son, Horus. Isis was the mother-

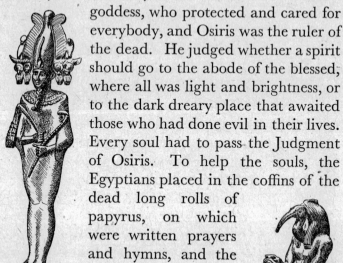

goddess, who protected and cared for everybody, and Osiris was the ruler of the dead. He judged whether a spirit should go to the abode of the blessed, where all was light and brightness, or to the dark dreary place that awaited those who had done evil in their lives. Every soul had to pass the Judgment of Osiris. To help the souls, the Egyptians placed in the coffins of the dead long rolls of papyrus, on which were written prayers and hymns, and the answers to be given to the questions which

Osiris

Osiris would ask when the soul stood before his judgment seat. These rolls, which have been found in many tombs of the Middle and the New Kingdom, have been put together by scholars in a collection which is called the Book of the Dead. One of the finest copies is to be seen in the British Museum.

Thoth

One of the gods who was worshipped in a special district was Ptah of Memphis. He was the creator of all things, even of the other gods, whom he said were his thoughts. He was often represented in the form of a mummy, leaning on a staff. In their idea of Ptah the Egyptians came near to the thought of God as a spirit, even though they portrayed him in a human form.

Many of the Egyptian gods are represented in the form of an animal, or as a human being with an animal head. Ra sometimes has a falcon's head. Hathor is often shown as a cow. Thoth, the god of wisdom, has the head of an ibis; Anubis, who watched over the embalming of the body and led the souls of the dead to the underworld, has a jackal's head. This curious practice arose from the fact that, in early times, the Egyptians thought certain animals were the symbols of certain gods. As people progressed they began to think of gods in human form, but as the less thoughtful ones still clung to the old animal forms, the priests joined the two together, and represented the gods as half human and half animal.

In the New Kingdom Amen, the god of Thebes, became the most important of the gods. It was he who had given victory to the Pharaohs in their wars; in return, they gave him many estates and built magnificent temples for him, so that his priests became rich and powerful. Then they wanted to make him god of the whole country, just as Marduk became the chief god throughout Babylonia in the time of Hammurabi. But the Egyptians, especially those who dwelt in the delta lands, did not want to forsake the worship of Ra. So, in order to gain these people as worshippers of Amen, the priests made the two gods into one, called Amen-Ra, and temples were built for his worship, not only throughout Egypt, but also in the other lands under Egyptian rule. Only once after this was the power of Amen-Ra disputed. This was when the Pharaoh Akhnaton tried to set up the worship of Aton. But the priests of Amen-Ra were too strong for him. After his death the worship of Aton came to an end, and Amen-Ra was all-powerful once more.

The temples of Amen-Ra at Thebes were the most magnificent in Egypt. One stood on the bank of the Nile, the other was in the northern part of the city. Between them ran a wide processional way flanked on either side by animal figures, with the body of a lion and the head of a ram. At the great festivals the priests bore the image of Amen-Ra down this road from one temple to the other, accompanied by musicians, singers and dancers, and a great crowd of people.

The central point in each temple was the dark chamber in which was placed the shrine of Amen-Ra, a wooden chest adorned with gold, silver, and jewels, like the Hebrew Ark of the Covenant. Only the priests might enter this inner chamber to perform the daily services of the god. His image was taken from its shrine, washed, clothed and anointed, and offered incense, food and drink, while prayers were recited and hymns of praise were sung. Around the shrine chamber were storerooms and vestries and, beyond these, colonnaded halls and courtyards where the people might gather. Most of these were not part of the original temples; they were built by great Pharaohs as thank-offerings to Amen-Ra for the victories he had granted them in war or the blessings he had bestowed on them in peace.

The skill of the finest craftsmen in Egypt was lavished on these halls and courtyards. Stone columns, with capitals carved into the shape of papyrus flowers or lotus buds, upheld the roof of the great hall of the northern temple, built by Ramses II, and each column was painted in bright colours with pictures of the gods and the Pharaohs. The sunlight, flooding in through the tall doorways at either end or falling in shafts through the barred windows under the roof, made this hall a medley of glowing colours. The walls of the courtyards and the massive gate towers were covered with carving and inscriptions, telling of the deeds of the Pharaoh who built them. Tall granite obelisks were set up to tell the same story. One of these stands to-day upon the Thames Embankment, and is known to us as Cleopatra's Needle. Huge statues of the Pharaohs stood around the courtyards and in front of the great entrance gates. No labour or expense was spared to

Where the Egyptians gathered to worship Amen-Ra

make the Theban temples the finest in the land, and even to-day, though the colours have faded and many of the columns and obelisks have fallen or been taken away, the ruins of these two temples tell us of the skill of the Egyptian masons, sculptors, and artists, and of the wealth and power of the Pharaohs of the Empire.

Beneath the cliffs on the other side of the Nile are the ruins of other temples. These were the tomb temples of the Pharaohs. In the days of the Empire they no longer built pyramids. Their tombs were hollowed out among the hills, in what is now called the Valley of the Kings. Among the rocky cliffs there was no room for tomb temples, so they were built in the flat land between the cliffs and the river. Here was once the temple of Amenhotep III, called the Magnificent. To-day the only remains of it are two enormous statues of the Pharaoh and his wife, which stood in front of the temple. The Greeks called these statues the " colossi of Memnon ". Here is still the temple of Queen Hatshepsut, the first woman ruler in history, who reigned about 1500 B.C. The walls of its colonnaded courtyards are covered with pictures, telling of the great trading expedition she sent to the land of Punt. They show the ships sailing down the Red Sea, the country through which the caravans passed, the Egyptian soldiers who protected it on its way, and the laden vessels discharging their cargoes of gold, ivory and incense, ostrich feathers, skins and slaves, which had then to be transported across the desert to Thebes.

Another fine temple is that of Ramses II, with its pictures of his campaigns in Syria and Palestine, and of the king himself doing great deeds in his chariot drawn by prancing horses. In the temple of Ramses III we see how the Egyptians fought at sea. A great relief there shows a battle between the ships of Ramses and the " People of the Isles ", the dwellers in the islands and coast lands of the Mediterranean Sea. As each Pharaoh died, his temple was added to those already standing, until this memorial city of the dead became the rival in grandeur of the city of the living on the other side of the river.

CHAPTER VIII

The craftsmen of Egypt

Boat-building was an important craft in Egypt. Metal-workers and jewellers made beautiful vessels and ornaments. The potters used a wheel to make their clay bowls. Weavers wove fine linen for clothes.

MOST of the stone-masons in Egypt were employed by the king, the priests, or the nobles on the building of tombs and temples. The finest artists and sculptors were also in their service, carving and painting pictures, making big granite statues, or smaller figures, such as that of a slave-woman rubbing corn between two stones, which is in the British Museum. But besides masons, artists, and sculptors, there were many craftsmen in Egypt who made the things needed in everyday life.

One of the most important crafts was boat-building. Roads in Egypt were simply sandy tracks, for it was not until the time of the Romans that people learned to make good roads. The Nile was Egypt's great highway. Traders bore their goods up and down the river ; nobles and officials used it for their business or their pleasure ; the Pharaoh travelled on it in his state barge ; even the gods themselves were rowed down it in their sacred boats at festivals. The boats used for all these purposes were made of wood, in much the same shape as the reed boats of the earliest Egyptians. They were curved upwards at each end to make the stern and the high prow, and provided with a mast, a sail, and a large oar for steering. A pleasure boat was gaily decorated in bright colours, and had a coloured awning in the middle to shield its owner from the heat of the sun.

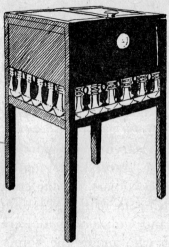

A chest made by an Egyptian carpenter

Other workers in wood were the carpenters. The most highly skilled made the wooden models placed in the tombs, and the beautiful carved and inlaid furniture which the wealthy Egyptians used. Others made instruments for agriculture, ploughs and sickles, spades and hoes. All these things, which to-day are made of iron and steel, were then made of wood, with copper or bronze fittings. Iron was not used in Egypt till the time of Ramses II, and then it was rare and costly.

Some of the most skilled craftsmen were the metal-workers. Workers in copper and bronze made

swords, battle-axes, spearheads, and daggers for the
soldiers, tools for the masons and sculptors, and

A jeweller's work

knives and household utensils. The silversmiths and
the goldsmiths made the beautiful vessels required
for the temple services, covered furniture in beaten

gold for the Pharaoh, and fashioned silver mirrors
and gold toilet articles for the rich Egyptian ladies.

There was always plenty of work for the jewellers,
for the Egyptians, both men and women, wore

much jewellery. Some of this has
been found in tombs like that of
Tutankhamen, a Pharaoh of the
Empire. Necklaces and bracelets
were made of amethyst, turquoise, carnelian, and lapis-lazuli,
or of gold inlaid with coloured enamels. Jewelled
pins and brooches served as fastenings for cloaks
and dresses. Rings were jewelled also, or of gold
and silver stamped with an in-
scription. These were used by
the Egyptians for sealing their
letters, just as we use signet rings
to-day. Gold fillets helped to
keep in place the heavy wigs
which both men and women
wore. An ornament belonging
specially to the Pharaoh was a

The inscription on the ring

pectoral, worn on the breast below the necklace.
Sometimes it was in the shape of a bird, and every
feather of the wings was made of a separate piece
of enamel or precious stone; sometimes it was a
square-shaped ornament, wrought in gold or inlaid
with precious stones. Nothing shows us better the
skill of the Egyptian craftsman than this finely

worked jewellery, made by hand, like that of the Sumerians, with only the simplest tools.

Among the oldest crafts were those of the vase-makers and potters. Beautiful stone vases, ground out by hand, were made by these men, as well as lamps of alabaster, ornamented with lotus flowers and figures of the gods, and ground to such thinness that the light from the wick, floating in the oil within the bowl, shone clearly through the sides. The potters made their clay bowls on a wheel. Some were plain and highly polished ; others were painted with animals, plants, and ships. The bowls of the Old Kingdom are more beautiful than those of later times. When metal became common, rich people used copper and bronze, and even gold and silver, for their tableware, so that clay pots were only used in the kitchen or by the poorer people.

A discovery which produced another craft was that of making glaze. This glaze was used for many pur- poses, for covering pottery, for colouring the little figures placed in hundreds in the tombs of the New Kingdom to perform tasks for the master after his death, for making beads for less expen-

An amulet

sive jewellery, and for the amulets which the Egyptians wore to shield them from the power of evil spirits. This glaze was of a rich blue or green colour. We do not know exactly how it was made. Many modern glaziers have tried to produce it, but they have never been able to find out the secret of the Egyptians.

Glass was not made in Egypt till the time of the New Kingdom. Even then it was very expensive, for the Egyptians did not know how to blow glass. They made their glass vessels by winding a thin string of glass round a sand core. In this way they could only make small articles, such as jars for holding perfumes and oils and the paint which both men and women used lavishly on their faces. Some of these are very beautiful, for the strings of glass were coloured blue and yellow, and then wound together round the core to make various patterns.

There were other crafts which gave employment to many workers. Numbers of men, the children of Israel among them, were employed in the brick-fields, for houses were built of brick, not stone. There were basket-makers and rope-makers, using for their wares palm leaves and reeds, and leather-workers turning out sandals, buckets and bottles, quilted leather caps and coats for soldiers, and coverings for shields. Weavers made the linen which was more suitable than wool for clothing in Egypt. In the Old and Middle Kingdoms men only wore short kilts, and women simple dresses like a short nightgown. In the New Kingdom an overdress was added, made of fine pleated linen, which required great skill for its weaving. Dyers and bleachers finished off the material when it was woven, making it snowy white or colouring it green and blue for women's dresses.

When Egypt was wealthy and prosperous, there was great demand for the work of the skilled craftsmen. Many of the materials which they needed had to be brought from other countries. The ships which left Egypt laden with corn and wine, linen and papyrus, brought back silver and copper, precious stones and fine woods. Caravans trading to Punt and Ethiopia returned with ivory and ebony, myrrh and spices, skins and ostrich feathers. As in Sumer and Babylon, the traders became an important class among the people. Many of the old Egyptian stories tell of the adventures which befell them on their journeys.

CHAPTER IX

Everyday life in Egypt

Many labourers were needed to till the fertile valley of the Nile. Rich men lived in spacious houses and had beautiful furniture. They amused themselves by hunting and giving parties.

Most of the poorer people in Egypt worked on the land, in the service of Pharaoh and the great nobles, or of the priests who managed the estates belonging to the temples. Often they were slaves, and even if they were freemen, there was not much difference in their position. They were not paid wages as a modern farm labourer is, for there was no coined money in Egypt. They were given a house, food, and clothing in return for their work. Their working days were from dawn to sunset, with a rest in the heat of the day ; for there was always plenty to do on the land, except in the flood season.

When the flood subsided, the fields were ploughed. Then the seed was scattered and trodden in by sheep and oxen. The shepherds sang as they drove the flocks across the sodden earth :

The shepherd is in the water among the fish,
He speaketh with the shad, and greeteth the . . . fish.

The growing crops had to be watered by means of the *shadûf*. This was a long pole, balanced on an upright beam, with a weight at one end and a skin bucket at the other. The bucket was pulled down and dipped in the river, which was now low, by a man standing on the brink, and then the weight at

the other end of the pole caused it to swing up to the man above, who was waiting to take it and pour the water into the canal which bordered the fields.

When harvest time came, the crops were reaped, threshed, and stored in the granaries. As each basketful was brought in, a scribe made a note of it on his papyrus roll. The storage bins were like large brick beehives ; at the top was a little door through which the corn was poured ; at the bottom was another little door through which it could be taken out.

Besides ploughing, sowing, and harvesting, the farm labourers had other tasks. The cattle had to be tended and the canals kept clean. The grapes had to be trodden in the winepress, and the wine bottled in tall jars with pointed ends, which were sunk in the earth in the master's storehouses. The barley had to be made into beer, the dates to be gathered, and the vegetable gardens cultivated. The fish in the river must be netted and the wild birds snared. Fish and game, with bread, fruit, and vegetables, were the chief articles of food. A labourer's life was hard ; but if he had a good master, it need not be unhappy. A good lord cared for his workers and saw that they had food and shelter, even in times of famine. Ameni, a rich noble, says, " No one was miserable in my community, no one ever hungered in my time ". Sometimes there were holidays, for, on the festivals of the gods, everybody went to the temple to watch the procession of the priests, or to the river to see the god pass down it in his sacred barge. Herodotus says that, on an occasion like this, the river was crowded with boats, filled with people playing flutes, shaking rattles, and singing and clapping their hands.

The houses in which the poor people lived were brick buildings, with three or four rooms and a staircase leading to the flat roof. They were not built round a courtyard like the Sumerian houses : they were more on the plan of a small modern house. The front door opened into an entrance room, which was used as a workshop or storeroom. It also served as sleeping quarters for the goat or the donkey and the geese and ducks, which by day were turned out in front of the house. Next to the entrance room was the living-room, and beyond this a bedroom and a

kitchen. These were cramped quarters for a whole family, but in the sunny Egyptian climate people lived out of doors a great deal. Women did their work on the roof or beside their front doors, and children played in the street just as they do in summer to-day.

A rich man's house was more spacious. It stood in its own grounds, of which part was a garden and part was occupied by granaries and storerooms, stables, kitchen, and servants' quarters. An entrance hall led into a long open gallery where the family could sit and enjoy the sunshine. From this a door opened into a spacious central room, in which the master of the house received his guests. Behind this were the private rooms of the family, a bedroom, bathroom, and dressing-room for the master, and sitting-rooms and bedrooms for his wife and children and their women slaves. A staircase led to the roof, part of which was covered with a richly decorated awning to make an open-air sitting-room.

The furniture in such a house was not unlike what we use to-day. There were beds with wooden

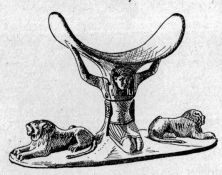

frames and carved heads; but instead of pillows, people used wooden head-rests. Chairs and stools were carved also, and sometimes inlaid with ivory and fine woods. There were no big tables, but stands

A rich man's head-rest

for holding food and drink. Gaily painted chests were used instead of wardrobes for storing clothes and valuables. In the kitchen quarters were cooking-vessels of clay or metal, drinking-cups and food-bowls, knives and spoons. In the reception room there was a brazier for a fire when the nights were cold, a stone trough and water-jar so that guests might wash their hands and feet on arrival, and mats on the floor, on which people sat if there were not enough chairs. In smaller houses people nearly always sat on the floor ; for poor people had little furniture beyond beds, one or two stools, and clay vessels for household use.

A rich man in Egypt had a pleasant and comfortable life. He spent part of his time looking after the affairs of his estate and going through his accounts with his steward, while one or more scribes sat round on the floor ready to enter all the particulars into the business rolls of the estate. Sometimes he went out into the desert with his dogs, to hunt gazelles and ibexes, or he went fishing and fowling among the marshes in a light skiff. On such expeditions his wife often went with him, and he took a cat to catch the birds that he brought down with his throwing-stick. If he got tired of these amusements, he could go to a bull-fight or a wrestling match. Much of his time was spent in giving and attending parties, where guests were entertained by acrobats, musicians, and dancers. In every large Egyptian household there were slaves to do all the work, so that the master and mistress had plenty of leisure. Even if a man were a royal official, he would still have time for recreation ; for the Pharaoh had such a number of people in his service that none of them had to work very hard.

CHAPTER X

The learning of the Ancient East

The Sumerians wrote on clay tablets. Their writing is called cuneiform. The Egyptians made hieroglyphics on papyrus. The ancient peoples told stories about gods and heroes.

EVERY boy and girl goes to school to-day. In Babylonia and Egypt only a few did so, and they were chiefly boys. If girls went to school at all, it was only to learn music and dancing, which were taught by the priestesses, so that they might take part in the festival processions of the gods. Boys, who were also taught in schools in the temple, learned reading, writing, arithmetic, and geometry. If they were going to be priests, they had to learn law, medicine, and astronomy, and the hymns and prayers to the gods as well. Arithmetic and geometry were important subjects, because they were necessary for laying out canals and calculating the boundaries of the fields, and, in Egypt, for measuring the rise of the Nile. Writing was a difficult art, at which schoolboys had to work very hard. The teacher's motto for lazy boys was, " The boy hath a back, he attends when it is beaten ".

The Sumerians were the earliest writers in the Land of the Two Rivers. Their writing was copied

The earliest writing

by Babylonians and Assyrians and all the people who lived around them. Even in Egypt letters have been found, written with the curious little wedge-shaped signs to which scholars have given the name of cunei-form. Before they reached the stage of actual writing, the Sumerians drew pictures if they wanted to make a record of any important act. A king who built a temple for his god would make a picture of a man with a crown, another of a house, and another of the god. But it took a long time to draw pictures for every-thing, so gradually the Sum-erians changed their draw-ings into signs. They used the sign for a certain sound wherever it occurred, whether it was the single

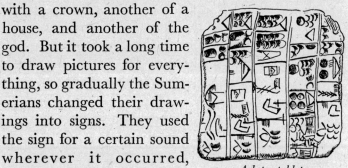

A later tablet

word for which they had used it in the first place, or in a longer word where it was only part of the whole. But they never made the signs stand for letters, so that they had no alphabet. Instead, they had long lists of sounds, and when they wanted to write a word, they put together the sound signs instead of putting together letters. To write on their clay tablets (for they had no paper), they used a bone or wooden stylus, like a three-sided pencil without a point. The writing was done while the clay was still damp, and then the tablet was baked. If it was a letter, it was often put in a clay envelope, which was addressed and sealed by the writer, and letter and envelope were baked together.

The Egyptian hieroglyphic writing began in the same way with pictures and sounds. The Egyptians, however, went a stage further and made their pictures stand for letters. But as they had no vowels, they had not a complete alphabet, and they still kept some of their word pictures. For instance, after a word which had to do with a human being, they drew a little man. The Egyptians could read this method of writing without any difficulty, though we do not find it so easy to-day when we want to read an inscription or a papyrus roll.

All the writing that has come down to us from the Old Kingdom is to be found on the walls of tombs and temples, for the Egyptians did not use clay tablets. But by the time of the Middle Kingdom, they had found a writing material something like paper. It was made from the pith of the thick stem of the papyrus plant. Strips were placed side by side vertically, then crossed with more strips horizontally, and the whole was pressed firmly together to make a thin sheet. A piece of any length could be made by gumming separate sheets together. After it was written on, it was rolled up and placed in a jar to keep it from injury.

The scribes who wrote on papyrus used a pointed reed, dipped in ink made from a mixture of red or black powder, gum, and water. They did not always

Part of the roll in the tomb of Ani

use the hieroglyphic script. Often they wrote in a hand that is called hieratic. In this writing the hieroglyphs were not fully made, so that the marks were more like signs than complete pictures. In time most of the Egyptian writing became hieratic, though the priests still used the hieroglyphic script in tombs and temples, and for the rolls that are now called the Book of the Dead. In later times a still simpler form of writing, called demotic, became common.

At first writing was used chiefly for business affairs. The Sumerians kept tablets of accounts, records of the size of their fields and the amount of their crops, bills of lading for trading vessels, and lists of goods sent by caravan to foreign lands. Egyptian scribes employed by a great noble kept careful account of the corn that was stored in a granary, the jars of wine produced from a vineyard, and the number of their master's cattle. The king's scribes kept records of the taxes that were paid, and wrote letters of instructions to his governors in different parts of the land. The priestly scribes, besides keeping the temple accounts, wrote tablets and rolls containing hymns and prayers to the gods, records of trials in their law courts, medical prescriptions, and spells for curing sickness. It was not until about 2000 B.C. that they began to write poetry and stories.

The ancient peoples told their stories and sang their poems, instead of writing them. Most of them were about the gods and kings and heroes of old. The Sumerians had a story about the creation of the world and another about a great flood, very like that in the Bible. Many people think that the Sumerian story and the Bible story both describe a flood that happened in Mesopotamia thousands of years ago. Another Sumerian story, that is inscribed on tablets which are now in the British Museum, is about a hero called Gilgamesh, who met with many adventures during his lifetime, fighting and conquering ogres

and wild animals, and journeying to the far places of
the earth. The Egyptians, too, had their story of the
Creation, and many stories of the gods. One of their
favourites told how Osiris came to be king of the
underworld. They also told fairy stories about mar-
vellous adventures that befell travellers and ship-
wrecked sailors, and about magicians who could
change men into trees or animals and pile up the
waters of a lake, as the waters of the Red Sea were
piled up for the Israelites.

Scribes were held in great honour, both in Mesopotamia and in Egypt. Fathers who wanted their
sons to get on in the world sent them to school in
order that they might become scribes, and gave them
advice such as the peasant Dwauf gave to his son
Pepi : " Set thine heart on books. . . . Would that I
might make thee love books more than thy mother."
No doubt Pepi's mother did not agree with her hus-
band about this.

CHAPTER XI

The Assyrian Empire

The Assyrian kings conquered many lands. They built cities and fine palaces. Assyrian sculptors could carve animals well.

AFTER the death of Hammurabi, the power of the Babylonian kings decreased, and about 1750 B.C. we find a new line of kings in Babylonia, belonging to a people called the Kassites. These Kassite kings ruled for nearly six hundred years. Then, in their turn, they had to fight against the Assyrians, who lived to the north of them in the valley of the Tigris. The chief city of the Assyrians was Ashur, which had paid tribute to Hammurabi. For some hundreds of years there was constant fighting between the rulers of Assyria and Babylon. By the time of Ashur-nasir-pal, who began to reign in 885 B.C., the victory of Assyria over Babylon was complete.

The Bible tells of the campaigns of the Assyrian kings in Syria and Palestine. It was not difficult to conquer these lands, for they were no longer defended by the strong rulers of Egypt or by the Hittite kings. Shalmaneser, the son of Ashur-nasir-pal, warred continually against the rulers of Syria, who

joined together against him under Ben-hadad, king
of Damascus, the chief of the Syrian cities. He also
took tribute from Jehu, king of Israel, who had
helped Ben-hadad. Eighty years later, another Shal-

THE ASSYRIAN EMPIRE
in the 7th. Century B.C.
English Miles
0   100 200 300 400 500

maneser fought against Hoshea, king of Israel, and
took Samaria, the chief Israelite city. Then only
Judah remained unconquered. In 700 B.C. Sennacherib set out to besiege Jerusalem. There he met
with a great disaster, which was probably due to an
outbreak of plague : " The angel of the Lord went
out, and smote in the camp of the Assyrian an
hundred fourscore and five thousand ; and when

they arose early in the morning, behold, they were all dead corpses ". In spite of this disaster, Hezekiah, king of Judah, had to pay tribute to Sennacherib. Finally the Assyrian kings conquered the once powerful Pharaohs of Egypt, so that Ashur-bani-pal, who became king of Assyria in 669 B.C., ruled the greatest empire of the ancient world.

The Assyrian kings won and kept their power by means of their armies. Their soldiers were armed

Chariots crossing a river

with swords, spears, and bows and arrows. Their weapons were often made of iron, a much harder metal than bronze. In battle an archer and a spearman fought together, the spearman protecting his comrade with his shield. They used wooden chariots, drawn by fleet horses, and battering-rams to besiege the enemy's walled cities.

The Assyrians were a fierce and cruel people, and often, after they had captured a city, they burned it to the ground. They tortured and killed many of the inhabitants or carried them off into slavery. Those that were left had to pay tribute of corn and cattle, wine and oil, and serve in the Assyrian armies.

The Assyrian kings were great builders. They built many cities in Assyria, the finest of which was Nineveh. It had double brick walls, with a moat running round the outer one. Inside the walls, raised on a mound above the houses and streets of

the city, were the palaces of the kings and the temples of the gods.

Both Sennacherib and Ashur-bani-pal built splendid palaces at Nineveh. They were of brick, richly decorated with coloured patterns and stone sculptures. On either side of the entrance were enormous winged figures with bodies of lions or bulls, and men's heads. The walls of the rooms were panelled with sculptured slabs, many of which are now in the British Museum. Some show the Assyrian armies marching, fighting, and besieging cities ; others show the king superintending the building of his palace, or amusing himself by hunting wild animals and fighting lions, a dangerous sport in which the Assyrians delighted.

The kings lived in great splendour. From Phoenicia they obtained a rich red dye, called Tyrian purple, for hangings and cushions, and for their long fringed and embroidered robes. From Syria came the cedar wood that clever craftsmen made into carved chairs and couches, and the copper and tin that metal-workers needed to make delicately engraved bronze bowls. From Elam came precious stones ; from Egypt, gold, ivory, and turquoise for ornaments and drinking-cups. The palace storerooms were full of meat, wine, and corn sent by the royal governors in the provinces for the great feasts that the king gave. Musicians and dancers attended at these feasts, for, like all ancient peoples, the Assyrians were fond of music.

Ashur-bani-pal, who died in 626 B.C., was a scholar as well as a soldier. In his palace was a large library stored with clay tablets and six-sided cylinders, written in the cuneiform script. On the cylinders were recorded the great deeds of the king both in war and peace. Many of the tablets were dictionaries. On others were written Sumerian hymns and prayers, which the Assyrians now sang in the temple of Ashur, their chief god. On other tablets were written the old stories of Babylonia ; it is from these that we know the stories of Gilgamesh and of the Flood.

There were tablets about astronomy and mathematics, lists of plants, and medical prescriptions. One of the prescriptions is for coughing ; licorice root is to be crushed and drunk in beer. Then there were tablets about chemicals and minerals, directions for making and colouring glass, and business contracts and letters, sealed in the Babylonian fashion. All the knowledge of the times was to be found in Ashurbani-pal's library. In a letter to one of his officers he says, " No one shall withhold tablets from thee, and if there be any tablet . . . which I have not mentioned to thee and thou shalt find it, and it is good for my palace, search for it and take it and send it to me ".

CHAPTER XII

Chaldeans and Persians

Nebuchadrezzar rebuilt the city of Babylon. Cyrus, the Persian king, captured it. Darius was " the great king ". Zoroaster taught that there was one supreme god.

" O KING OF ASSYRIA, thy nobles shall dwell in the dust ; thy people is scattered upon the mountains." In 612 B.C. these words of Nahum, the prophet of Judah, came true. The Medes and Chaldeans marched on Nineveh and burnt it to the ground. The Assyrian Empire fell. The Median ruler took the parts of it surrounding his own territories, and the rest became the kingdom of the Chaldeans.

The greatest of the Chaldean kings was Nebuchadrezzar (called Nebuchadnezzar in the Bible). He had much fighting to do during his reign, for his subjects rebelled against him. They were supported by Pharaoh Necho, whom Nebuchadrezzar defeated at Carchemish. But Nebuchadrezzar is remembered not so much for his victories in war as for his rebuilding of the city of Babylon, which he made the capital of his kingdom. Herodotus, who visited the city about one hundred and fifty years later, says that it was in the form of a square, each side of which was fifteen miles long. Excavators, who have dug out the foundations of the walls, say it was not really as big as this; but it was much bigger than any other city of ancient times.

Quays, streets, and houses lay on both sides of the river. The part of the city on the left bank was surrounded by a double brick wall. The space between the outer and inner wall was filled in with earth, so that it formed a broad road, with covered walks on either side and room for a four-horse chariot between them. Inside this area was the king's palace. It was not, like the palaces of the Assyrian kings, adorned with stone sculptures. Instead, the walls were covered with patterns and pictures in blue, yellow, and red. They were made by applying coloured glaze to the brickwork, an art in which the Babylonians were skilled and which is still practised to-day.

The gardens which Nebuchadrezzar made in his palace grounds, to give pleasure to his queen, were said by the Greeks to be one of the Seven Wonders of the World. They called them the Hanging Gardens of Babylon, because they were lifted so far above the buildings around them that they appeared to hang from the sky. In reality they were made on a number of terraces, built on brick arches one on top of the other. Soil was heaped on these terraces to such a depth that flowers and shrubs, and even small trees, could be planted in it. In the hot Babylonian sunshine, the cool recesses under the arches and the shady walks in the gardens must have been very pleasant.

Nebuchadrezzar paid honour to Marduk, the ancient god of the city, by making a great processional road from his palace to the temple-tower of

Babel. The square paving-stones of this road, along which the king passed with the statue of the god on his great festival, can still be seen among the ruins of the city.

The entrance to the road near the palace was by a double gateway, with brick towers on either side. Like the walls of the palace, they were covered with coloured glaze, and in addition they were decorated with figures of animals, made in brick. Each brick had to be carefully moulded, so that when it was put into its place it would help to form the whole animal. The animals shown were the bull, which was a sacred animal in the east, and a fanciful creature that we can call a dragon. The bricks of the wall were coloured bright blue, while the bulls were yellow and the dragons white.

It was to this city that Nebuchadrezzar brought the people of Judah when he carried them away captive from Jerusalem in 586 B.C., because they had rebelled against him. There " by the rivers of Babylon " they would meet many other strangers and captives, for the city was built largely by the people of the lands the king had conquered. It was perhaps in the great throne-room of the palace that Belshazzar saw the writing on the wall that we read about in the Book of Daniel.

The glory of Babylon did not last long after the death of Nebuchadrezzar. His successors were weak kings, and enemies gathered round on all sides. The chief of these were the Persians, who had united with the Medes and built up an empire to the north and east of Babylonia. The Persian ruler, Cyrus, coveted the rich lands of the river valley. In 539 B.C. he attacked Babylon. Belshazzar, the son of King Nabonidus, and the commander of the Babylonian army, could not withstand him. Babylon was not burnt to the ground as Nineveh had been ; it became instead one of the largest and most populous cities of the Persian Empire.

The Persian Empire was even larger than the Assyrian Empire. Eastwards it extended almost to the borders of India, and in the west Cyrus added to it the kingdom of Lydia and the Greek cities on the coast of Asia Minor, as well as the territories of the Chaldean kings. His son, Cambyses, conquered Egypt. Cambyses planned to make a Persian empire in Africa as well as Asia, but he was recalled to his own country by the news of a rebellion there. Before he could reach Persia he died, and it was left to Darius, who succeeded him, to subdue the rebellion and restore peace throughout his dominions.

We know the achievements of Darius from his great sculpture on a rock at Behistun, beside the caravan road from Babylon to Ecbatana, the capital of the old Median kingdom. It shows seven rebel chieftains brought before the king in chains, and underneath it is inscribed in cuneiform writing a record of his great deeds. This record was in three languages, Persian, Susian (the language of the ancient Elamites), and Babylonian, so that all the soldiers and officials, the traders and the travellers who used the road, might read of the might of Darius, " the great king, king of kings, king of the lands ".

The Persian rulers adopted many of the customs of the people they conquered. Their dress was like that of the Assyrians, even to their stiffly curled hair

I   G

and beards. The royal palaces were ornamented
with glazed and coloured bricks in the Babylonian
manner, and the wide stairways which led to the
platforms on which they stood were adorned with
sculptures, like the palaces of the Assyrian kings.
Their soldiers were equipped with bows and arrows,
iron swords, shields and spears, like the Assyrians
and Babylonians. They carried on trade in the
same way, bringing to Susa and Persepolis cedar

A sculpture on the palace stairway

from Lebanon, gold from Asia Minor, silver from
Egypt, ivory and precious stones from India and
the eastern provinces of the empire. But they were
not as cruel and oppressive as the Assyrian rulers.
They allowed the people they conquered to live in
peace, to worship their own gods and to use their
own language, provided they obeyed their Persian
governor, and paid the tribute he demanded of
them. Cyrus sent the Jews, whom Nebuchadrezzar
had carried captive to Babylon, back to their own
land, and allowed them to rebuild the city of
Jerusalem and the temple of Yahweh.

It may have been their religion which made the Persian rulers more just and merciful than the Assyrian kings. In early times the Persians, like all other peoples of the East, worshipped many gods; but in the time of Cyrus there lived a prophet called Zoroaster, who taught that there was one supreme god, Ahura Mazda, "the wise Lord". He was the creator of all good things and the teacher of men, demanding of his followers "the well-thought thought, the well-spoken word, and the well-done deed". But there were also spirits of evil, chief of whom was Ahriman, who was responsible for all wrong-doing in the world. Ahura Mazda was, however, more powerful than Ahriman, and in the end he would triumph and evil would be vanquished. This religion encouraged men to do good deeds, because in this way they would please Ahura Mazda, enjoy the warmth and light that he gave to men through the fire that was his outward sign, and go to his kingdom of good and happiness after death. In some ways the teaching of Zoroaster is like that of the Hebrew prophets concerning Yahweh: "I desired mercy and not sacrifice; and the knowledge of God more than burnt offerings". And though Zoroaster lived more than five hundred years before Jesus Christ, he taught, like Him, that good deeds were better than wealth and power.

CHAPTER XIII

The civilization of Crete

The people of Crete were seamen and traders. They made beautiful pottery. The Minos lived in a wonderful palace. The Minoans worshipped a snake-goddess.

To the north of Egypt, in the Mediterranean Sea, lies the island of Crete. Its backbone is a mountain ridge, from which spurs run down to the sea, enclosing fertile sun-warmed valleys. Here, when the Pharaohs were raising their great pyramids, another race was building up a civilization of its own. The Cretans differed from both Egyptians and Semites ; they belonged to what is called the Mediterranean race. We do not know how long they had lived in the island. The earliest inhabitants were, as in other lands, a stone-using people ; but about 3000 B.C. they discovered copper, which they soon learned to mix with tin to make bronze. Then they made rapid progress in agriculture and craftsmanship.

Like every other people, the Minoans, as the early inhabitants of Crete are often called, were first of all occupied with gaining food, shelter, and clothing. There was plenty of stone in the island, so they built houses of two or more storeys, generally with foundations and lower parts of stone and the rest of brick and timber. The women wove cloth from the wool of the sheep that they pastured on the hillsides, while the men went fishing off the coasts and gathered the olives and figs that grew in abundance in the hot sunshine.

But there was little suitable land for growing corn. Even though the inhabitants used every inch of the fertile valleys, their supplies of wheat and barley were always perilously scanty. The need for more corn led the Minoans to become a trading people. They converted their frail fishing-boats into stout wooden vessels, equipped with sails and oars ; and soon the Mediterranean Sea was alive with Cretan ships, bringing from Egypt and Asia and the neighbouring islands, not only food, but also materials for use in industry. Copper and tin for bronze tools and weapons, corn and timber to eke out the island supplies, silver, linen, and perfumes for the richer classes filled the holds of the Cretan vessels and provided materials for the labour of the Cretan craftsmen. The Minoans handled their vessels so skilfully that they won great renown as sailors among their neighbours. Soon they went farther afield, and began to carry the wares of other people, as well as their own, for bartering at the ports at which they touched. Thus they created a new industry and became the first carriers of the sea.

In the making of pottery the Cretan craftsmen excelled those of any other people of their time. They moulded the clay on their wheels into the finest shapes, and then ornamented it with elaborate, beautifully drawn patterns. Buff-coloured pots were painted in red and yellow, with designs of coral and seaweed, shell-fish and the tentacled octopus. Tall vases were covered completely with black paint, on which were shown slender white lilies and the irises and crocuses which bloom in the valleys in spring. Vases such as these have been found in other countries as well as in Crete, carried there by the Minoan traders for exchange in the marketplace or by the envoys of the Minoan kings for gifts to neighbouring rulers.

A Minoan town was generally built a short distance from the sea and connected with its harbour by a road paved with stone boulders. In the largest town, Knossos, was the palace of the Minos, the chief priest and ruler of the island. Through the excavations which an English archaeologist has carried on for forty years, we have learned much about the palace and the life that was lived in it about 1500 B.C.

The palace occupied the top of the hillock on which Knossos stood, three miles from the northern coast of the island. Its buildings were grouped round a paved courtyard, with an entrance passage and gateway on the side towards the sea. In the block on the left of the courtyard were the royal apartments and the workshops of the king's craftsmen. The rooms in which the king and queen and their family lived were approached by a wide stone staircase, leading down from the courtyard, for on this side the ground sloped so sharply that there were two storeys below the courtyard level. Some of the rooms had windows looking out over the open valley; others were lighted by means of big open shafts from above. The walls, even those of the bathrooms, were gaily painted ; the ceilings were supported by graceful pillars ; and carved stone or wooden benches ran round the walls. Skin rugs covered the benches, and embroidered hangings draped the doorways.

The workmen's quarters were a maze of passages, out of which opened small rooms, fitted up with metal-workers' furnaces, kilns and potters' wheels, carpenters' and stone-cutters' benches, and goldsmiths' bronze tools. Here were made all the things needed for the royal household, as well as the wares which formed the cargo of the royal trading vessels.

On the western side of the courtyard were the king's throne-room, the offices for his ministers and scribes, and the storerooms in which he kept his dues of corn, wine, and oil, and the goods which he gained by trade. Stone storage-jars for oil, each large enough to hold a grown man, have been found in this part of the palace, as well as brick-lined cavities in the floors which served as safes. These storerooms opened on to another courtyard, in which the asses which carried the goods to and from the harbour could be loaded and unloaded.

On this side of the palace also was the theatre, a stone-paved arena with tiers of steps on two sides, which were used as benches. Here the Minos would sit, with his courtiers around him, to watch dancing and other pastimes, or to receive foreign envoys and the tribute of his subjects.

The pictures which covered the walls of the palace tell us something about Minoan life. They were not, like the Egyptian pictures, coloured carvings ; they were frescoes, that is, paintings in colour on a plaster background. Among them are pictures of birds with gorgeous plumage among the trees, and of fish in the sea, a boy gathering flowers, and a prince surrounded by tall white lilies. A picture of a banquet shows the dress of the Cretan men, an embroidered kilt held in place by a broad metal belt, high boots or leggings, silver ornaments, an engraved dagger, and a seal-stone, set in a ring or worn like a wrist-watch. Another picture shows the sport in the bull-ring, where nimble youths and girls caught the infuriated bull by the horns and turned somersaults over his back.

The mother-goddess of the Minoans

By permission of Macmillan & Co.

It was a sport that needed courage as well as speed, and was a popular spectacle among the Cretans.

We know little about the laws and the religion of the Minoans, for no one has yet been able to read their writing. It is neither cuneiform nor hieroglyphic, nor is it like the later Greek writing. We know they worshipped a goddess in whose care were all living things, for statuettes of her have been found. She holds in her hands the snake which was her emblem, and wears the dress of a Cretan lady, a flounced skirt and a small apron, a short-sleeved, low-necked bodice, drawn tightly in at the waist, and a tall cap, like an inverted flower-pot. Some people think that the legend of the Minotaur shows that they also worshipped a bull-god. We know too that the Minoans cared for their dead, for stone-built chamber tombs, similar to the cliff tombs of Egypt, have been found. The temple tomb of the priest-kings has also been discovered. Apparently they had good laws. There is a story that a Minos was made judge in Hades, because of the justice of his sentences on earth. Of their own stories we know nothing, though we have many stories about them, told by people who came after them.

The life of the Minoans was peaceful, for their swift sailing-vessels and their skilled sailors kept them safe from invasion. But they had one enemy which no skill could withstand, the earthquakes which laid low their cities again and again. About 1400 B.C.

the palace of Knossos was destroyed for the third time, and it was never rebuilt. But though the great day of Crete was over, Minoan arts and crafts did not perish completely, for they had already been copied by the people who lived on the mainland. In later times the Greeks built their theatres like the theatre at Knossos ; they adorned the walls of their public buildings with frescoes, and carried on the Cretan tradition of painted pottery. Lycurgus, the lawgiver of Sparta, was said by the Greeks to have studied the laws of Crete, and Zeus, the father of the Greek gods, was thought to have been born on Mount Ida. In ways like these the Minoan civilization helped to build up the still greater civilization of the Greeks, to which we trace much of what is best in the life of to-day.

CHAPTER XIV

The world of Homer

The Mycenaeans farmed the valleys of Greece. They were traders and craftsmen. Their kings and nobles were warriors. Homer's poems tell about their warfare with the Trojans.

MOST children know the stories from the *Odyssey*, a poem composed by Homer nearly three thousand years ago. Beside the *Odyssey*, Homer composed the *Iliad*, which tells of the warfare between the people of Troy and an army of invaders from across the sea. Ever since Homer composed his poems, people have delighted in them. About a hundred years ago, a German boy, Heinrich Schliemann, learned them almost by heart, and then it became his great desire to see the cities that were talked about in the *Iliad*. They had completely disappeared in the centuries that had passed since Homer's time, but Schliemann believed he knew where to find them. He worked hard and saved money, and when he was forty-eight he was able to start digging at a place called Hissarlik in Asia Minor, on a hill overlooking the Dardanelles. In the course of his excavations he found the remains of nine cities, one of which was the fortified city in which had lived the Trojans of Homer's story. He also went to Greece, where he found the remains of Mycenae, the city of Aga- memnon, the leader of the invading host.

Like Crete, Greece is a land of mountain ridges ending at the coast in rocky headlands, between which are wide bays and deep inlets. Little rivers flow down the valleys between the hills, and on the banks of these, usually near the mouth, the earliest inhabitants of Greece made their homes. Like the Minoans, they cultivated the soil in the valleys, and pastured their cattle and grew olives and grapes on the hillsides. In some ways their life was simpler than that of the Minoans. Each family dwelt in its farmhouse among the fields, a house consisting chiefly of one large room or hall, round which were barns and storehouses, byres and sheep-pens. If the farm was a small one, the farmer and his family tilled it themselves. Larger farmers had servants, who lived in the farmhouse as part of the family.

In the midst of the farms was the fortress, set on a low hill or rocky height, and enclosed by a wall built of huge blocks of stone. At Mycenae the gate- way was formed by two massive stone posts, across which a third was laid to form the top. It was set back at the end of a narrow passage between high walls, so that it could be defended in case of attack. The kings of Mycenae, unlike the rulers of Crete, needed strong walls for defence, for their kingdom lay on a neck of land, across which ran a road from sea to sea. They gained great wealth from the tribute paid by traders for using this road, and so were liable to attacks from envious neighbours. Within the fortress walls was space enough for the people who dwelt in the valley around to find refuge, with their goods and cattle, in time of war.

The king's palace stood in the middle of the fortified enclosure. Like the Minoan palace, it was built round a courtyard, but it was simpler in plan. Its large hall served as court, place of justice, and banqueting-room, and also as sleeping quarters for soldiers and passing travellers. The timbered roof was upheld by tall wooden pillars; in the middle was a stone hearth, above which was a hole in the roof for the smoke to escape. Wooden benches ran

round the walls, which were hung with shields, spears, and helmets. Around the courtyard were kitchens and storerooms, with a separate block for the women of the king's household.

Besides being farmers, the Mycenaeans were also traders and craftsmen. They adorned their buildings with sculpture and painting. They made carved furniture and gold and silver vessels, decorated with raised patterns of fruit and flowers or hunting and battle scenes. Their bronze weapons and shields were engraved and inlaid, and their pottery was painted after the fashion of the Minoans. They wore finely wrought gold and silver jewellery. The women, from the queen and her ladies downwards, were skilled weavers and embroiderers. Some of the beautiful things found by excavators may actually have been made by Minoan craftsmen, for the Minoan ships were often to be seen in Mycenaean harbours. But most of them were the work of the Mycenaeans themselves, who were clever with their hands and soon learned to copy the work of the Minoans. They sailed the sea in ships like those of the Minoans, exporting their wine, wool, and olives and bringing back gold, silver, tin, and the other materials they needed.

Mycenae and its neighbouring cities, such as Argos and Sparta, grew up about the same time as Crete. They were wealthy and flourishing cities between 1600 and 1200 B.C. But the rulers of Crete seem to have been more powerful than the mainland kings and to have exercised a kind of lordship over them. In later times the Greeks told the story of Theseus, one of a band of noble youths and maidens sent yearly as a sacrifice to a fearsome monster, the Minotaur, who had his lair in the palace of Knossos. Perhaps this story is a remembrance of a time when the mainland cities paid tribute to Crete. But when

Knossos was destroyed, the Mycenaeans took the place of the Minoans as the chief people of the Mediterranean. Their power, however, did not last long, for barbarian tribes from the north invaded the land. They soon overcame the Mediterranean people, and either killed or enslaved the men, and took the

Theseus slaying the Minotaur

women to be their wives. Then they settled in the cities and their chieftains became kings in their turn.

It was of these invaders, whom he calls Achaians, that Homer tells in his poems. Even when settled in the Mycenaean cities, they did not become farmers and traders, but used the labour of the conquered Mycenaeans for these purposes. They still thought warfare the finest of all occupations and looked upon renown in battle as the highest honour. Troy was only one among many places that they attacked round the shores of the Aegean Sea. Greek legends say that the Trojan war began because Paris, the son of Priam, king of Troy, had carried off Helen, the beautiful wife of Menelaus, king of Sparta. Menelaus called upon the Achaian princes to help him rescue Helen and punish Paris. Agamemnon, king of Mycenae, was made leader of the expedition. Under him were many other kings and princes, each

An inlaid dagger-blade

leading his own men. They laid siege to Troy, but the city was stoutly defended by the Trojan warriors. The *Iliad* tells of only a short part of the siege, during which Achaian and Trojan heroes used to fight each other single-handed, while the others looked on. The greatest of these combats was that in which Achilles, the most renowned of the Achaians, vanquished Hector, the finest warrior in the Trojan host. Homer's poem ends with a description of the burial of Hector :

Thus spake he, and they yoked oxen and mules to wains, and quickly then they flocked before the city. So nine days they gathered great store of wood. But when the tenth moon rose with light for men, then bare they forth brave Hector, weeping tears, and on a lofty pyre they laid the dead man, and thereon cast fire.

But when the daughter of Dawn, rosy-fingered Morning, shone forth, they gathered the folk around glorious Hector's pyre. First quenched they with bright wine all the burning, so far as the fire's strength went, and then his brethren and his comrades gathered his white bones lamenting, and big tears flowed down their cheeks. And the bones they took and laid in a golden urn, shrouding them in soft purple robes, and straightway laid the urn in a hollow grave and piled thereon great close-set stones, and heaped with speed a barrow. . . . And when they had heaped the barrow they went back, and gathered them together and feasted right well in noble feast at the palace of Priam, Zeus-fostered king.

Thus held they funeral for Hector, tamer of horses.

After ten years the struggle ended with the victory of the Achaians, who, so the story goes, made a wooden horse which they filled with soldiers and induced the Trojans to draw within their walls. When night came, the Achaian soldiers opened the gates for their comrades, who sacked the city and took captive all the high-born youths and beautiful women. Then they sailed for home, and the *Odyssey* tells of the voyage of Odysseus, and of the adventures that befell him before he reached his home in Ithaca.

Though Homer was not writing history, we can learn much about the life of the earliest Greeks from his poems. We see them at home and in the camp; we read of their ships and their armour, their feasts and their way of worshipping their gods. We know how their old men met together in council to advise the king, and how their young men tried to outdo one another in feats of daring and in sporting contests. We see also how the early Greeks adopted many of the Mycenaean customs, and how, because of this, the beginnings of their civilization are to be traced to Mycenaean as well as Minoan influence.

CHAPTER XV

How the Greek cities grew and multiplied

The Greeks were skilled sailors. They founded many cities round the shores of the Mediterranean Sea. The nobles governed the cities. The Greeks used money to carry on trade.

HOMER's Achaians were not the only invaders of the Mediterranean lands. Other tribes, akin to them, came with them or after them, settling on the Greek mainland, in the islands of the Aegean Sea, and on the coasts of Asia Minor. No one knows how long the invasions went on, nor exactly what befell; for in times of warfare men cannot make songs or write history. But the Aegean world about 800 B.C. was very different from the world of the Minoans and Mycenaeans.

The Dorians were the strongest and most numerous of the invading tribes. They used iron weapons, and they seem to have been barbarians when they arrived in Greece. They cared little for comfort and beauty, and much for warfare and plunder. So they destroyed most of the things which Homer describes in the *Iliad*. A poet called Hesiod tells us of the time in which he lived, about one hundred years after Homer. He says, " Now verily is a race of iron. Neither by day shall they ever cease from weariness and woe, neither in the night from wasting and sore cares." He describes the farmer as having only a small piece of land, with a simple wooden plough, one ox, and one servant to help him. Clothing was unadorned, food was scanty, and people had to work long hours all the year round. Their only holidays were after the harvest and the vintage. This is a different story from that of Homer. But Hesiod was writing about poor people, whereas Homer was describing princes and nobles.

The Greeks did not long remain simple farmers and warriors. Quite early they changed from farm to city life, living in the old Mycenaean cities, though still tilling the land that belonged to them outside. By degrees, the wealthier farmers ceased to do their own work, for slaves were easy to obtain. Moreover, the high-born men of the community had other things to occupy their time. It was their task to govern the city. When the Greeks first came into the land, each tribe had its own leader or king ; but during the centuries about which we know little, the kings disappeared, and about 800 B.C. the nobles were both the largest landowners and the rulers in the cities. If the ordinary people met together in an assembly, they could only agree with the decisions of the nobles. Such a form of government is called an aristocracy. It was the form which was usual in the Greek cities as we first see them.

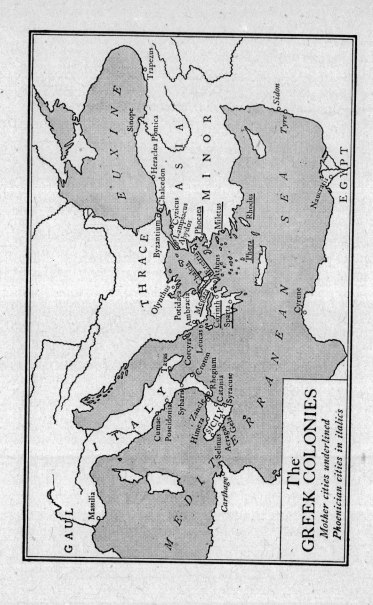

The
GREEK COLONIES

Mother cities underlined
Phoenician cities in italics

Beside the landowners, there were many traders and craftsmen in the cities. For with the coming of peace, the Greeks increased rapidly in numbers, and soon they found their valleys too small to feed them comfortably. Then, like the Minoans and Mycenaeans, they took to trade. But before they could become a great trading people they had to struggle with the Phoenicians, who had taken the place of the Minoans and Mycenaeans as the carriers of the sea. The chief Phoenician cities were Tyre and Sidon, at the eastern end of the Mediterranean; but by 800 B.C. they had founded many other trading settlements, the most famous of which was Carthage, on the coast of North Africa. Their ships sailed all round the Mediterranean and beyond the Pillars of Hercules, the ancient name for the Straits of Gibraltar. It is said that they even came to the shores of our own land in search of tin. Their trade made them rich and prosperous, so they were alarmed when they found the swift vessels of the Greeks competing with their slower, heavier ships, and taking from them the chief source of their wealth. Matthew Arnold, a poet of the nineteenth century, describes how the Phoenician trader

saw the merry Grecian coaster come,
Freighted with amber grapes, and Chian wine,
Green bursting figs, and tunnies steep'd in brine;
And knew the intruders on his ancient home,
The young light-hearted Masters of the waves.

The Greek trader was not only a merry fellow, he was also an enterprising and clever sailor. Soon the Greeks beat the Phoenicians in seafaring, and traders became an important class in every Greek city.

When the space within the walls of a city became overcrowded and the land outside fully occupied, bodies of citizens were sent out to form colonies in other lands. Miletus, the wealthiest of the cities of Ionia, on the coast of Asia Minor, founded more than sixty colonies round the shores of the Hellespont and the Euxine (which are now called the Dardanelles and the Black Sea). She also helped to found Naucratis in Egypt. Megara, a Dorian city, established Byzantium, famous in later history as Constantinople, and now called Istanbul. Other colonists went westward. Corinth, another Dorian city, founded Syracuse in Sicily. The heel and toe of Italy were dotted with Greek colonies. By 600 B.C. the Greek world extended far beyond Greece itself.

Each colony was founded on the same plan as its mother-city. It was built in the same way; it had the same form of government and worshipped the same gods. In time of danger it looked to the mother-city for help. At first the colonists had to obtain from their mother-city everything they needed, even food and clothing. But soon they set up their own industries, and became as great trading centres as the old cities. This often led to quarrels, but even so, the colonists never quite forgot their parent cities and the ties that bound them to one another.

In the seventh century B.C. the Greeks learned the use of coined money. Barter, the method of exchange by which early trade was carried on, was a clumsy way of buying and selling. The people of the Ancient East had improved upon it by using, as a form of money, sacks of barley, lumps of silver and gold rings.

A Lydian coin   *A Greek coin*   *A Persian coin*

But this " money " was not very convenient, and the Lydians replaced it by metal coins. These were copied by the Greeks, and soon every city had its own coinage, stamped with its own device. That of Athens, for example, had the head of Athena on one side, and the owl, which was her emblem, on the other. Since the time of the Greeks, all civilized people have used a coinage of some kind. Thus, though the Greeks did not actually invent money, they spread the use of it so widely that it may be placed among the useful things we owe to them.

CHAPTER XVI

The gods of Greece

The Greek gods dwelt on Mount Olympus. Zeus was the father of the gods. The Games were festivals in which all Greeks joined.

TO-DAY we think of ourselves first of all as Englishmen, and secondly as citizens of London or Manchester. Among the Greeks it was just the opposite. Each man thought of himself first as a citizen. His city played the most important part in his life, coming even before his home and his family. Pericles, one of the greatest citizens of Athens, said, " It is but natural that all of us . . . should wish to spend ourselves in her service ". Every Greek had this feeling for his city.

But though the Greeks did not think of themselves as a nation, they had certain things in common which made them different from people of another country, such as Egypt or Persia. One of these was their religion. They all worshipped the same gods. Like the people of the Ancient East, the Greeks had many gods. Zeus was the father of the gods. He had a wife, Hera, and a family of children, Athena, Apollo, Artemis, Hermes, and others. His brothers were

Hades, king of the underworld, and Poseidon, who ruled the sea as Zeus ruled the earth.

Each of these gods and goddesses had some special characteristic. Apollo was the god of light and youth. Hermes, with little wings on his heels, was the swift-

Poseidon, Apollo, and Artemis

footed messenger of the gods. Artemis, with her bow and arrow, was the goddess of the chase. Athene was the serious-eyed goddess of wisdom ; Hephaestus was the blacksmith who made armour and weapons for the gods ; Ares was the god of war. There were lesser gods too. One whom every countryman knew was Pan, the goat-footed god of Nature, who could be heard at evening playing sweet tunes on his reed pipes.

Some of the gods had particular places under their protection, where they were specially worshipped. Athens was the city of Athena, as Argos was of Hera. Apollo had his shrine at Delphi. But this did not prevent them from being worshipped in other places as well. Hera and Athena were prayed to for help, not only by Argives and Athenians, but by all the other Greeks. Zeus, as the father of the gods, was the protector and helper of all.

The Greeks thought that in many ways the gods were like men. Zeus and his family lived together on Mount Olympus. They ate and slept, and even fought like mortals. Sometimes, like a human family, they quarrelled among themselves, and the children were rude and disobedient to their parents. They had their favourites among mortals too. In Homer's story of the fight between Achilles and Hector, Achilles won because he was specially helped by Athena.

But the gods were much more powerful than men. On them depended the crops, the olive and the vine harvest, safety on the sea, success in battle and happiness at home. So the Greeks worshipped them with prayer and sacrifice. In every house there was a shrine, and an altar on which gifts of oil and wine and honey were placed. Here the father of the family offered daily prayers to the gods. In the temples the priests offered sacrifices and the people gathered together for worship. Each city had its religious festivals which were the holidays of the citizens. In the country the greatest festival took place in spring, which was the beginning of the year in ancient times. According to the Greek story, Kore, the daughter of Demeter, the goddess who watched over all growing things, was carried off by Hades to the dark underworld. Once every year he allowed Kore to return to earth, and the joy of her mother was shown in the return of life and growth in the world after the long cold winter. When the trees began to show leaf and the green blades to spring from the earth, the Greeks held their festival in honour of Demeter, bringing her offerings of barley cakes, cheese and honey, and fresh water from a sacred spring, praising her for the new year and praying her to bless the fruits of the earth.

There were four great festivals, called the Games, to which Greeks from every city came. At these, beside religious rites, there were athletic contests, in which every free-born Greek could compete. These contests formed part of the festival because the Greeks believed strongly in the importance of having healthy bodies. They loved beauty, and they thought that people should be beautiful as well as things. So they encouraged bodily exercise of every kind. In school boys were trained in gymnastics, and when they grew up they continued to exercise on the city sports ground. The best athletes were selected to be the champions of the city at the Games.

Where the citizens of Poseidonia worshipped Demeter

The oldest Games were those held in honour of Zeus at Olympia. Once in every four years the quiet grove beneath the wooded hill of Cronos, where his sanctuary stood, was alive with bustle and excitement. Children played by the rippling waters of the Cladeus and Alpheus ; young men exercised in the gymnasium ; and their elders lounged in the porticoes built to shelter the pilgrims during the five days of the festival. The Games began with a service before the altar of Zeus. Then the people crowded into the stadium, a long enclosure surrounded by tiers of seats, such as we see, copied from the Greek model, in some of our big towns. The most important contest

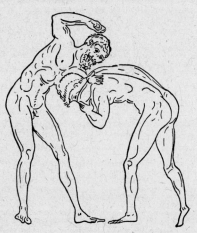

At the Games

here was the *pentathlon*, a series of five events : jumping, wrestling, running, throwing the disc, and hurling the javelin. There was also a separate foot-race, and another wrestling match. Horse-races and chariot-races took place in the hippodrome, and the festival ended with musical competitions and verse-reciting. At Olympia the only reward given to the victor in a contest was a wreath of wild olive, but on his return home he would be fêted and given rich gifts, for he had gained honour for his city as well as renown for himself.

Beside the Olympic Games, there were the Pythian Games before Apollo's shrine at Delphi, the Isthmian Games at Corinth in honour of Poseidon, and the Nemean Games in Argos. At Delphi the victor's crown was of bay leaves, at Corinth and Argos of wild parsley. Pindar, a poet of Thebes, who wrote songs in honour of the victors in the Games, tells us of a Corinthian athlete who had won all four crowns :

> For victor in the Contests Five is he
>   And in the foot-race ; so hath he attained
> Such glory multiplied of victory
>   As mortal never yet before hath gained.
> And shadowed was his head by garlands twain
>   When Isthmus saw him win the parsley meed.
> Kindness no less from Nemea did he gain.
>   The record of his father's lightning speed
> Is treasured still where Alpheus softly paces.
>   Yea, and at Pytho by his feet were won
> The crowns of honour in the two-fold races,
>   Single and double, under one day's sun.

These festivals helped greatly towards making the Greeks feel they were one people. During the month in which a festival was held, all quarrels between cities ceased. Men from every city joined in the worship of a god in whose care they all were. They spoke the same language, and heard together the songs of Homer, whom all alike revered. They all praised the achievement of a great athlete and delighted in the music of a beautiful poem. For a time, at least, the Greeks forgot the things that separated them and enjoyed the things that united them.

CHAPTER XVII

Athens and Sparta

Athens and Sparta were the leading cities in Greece. The Athenian citizens helped to govern their city. Every Spartan citizen was trained to be a good soldier.

BETWEEN 800 and 600 B.C. the Greeks established colonies in other lands, and became the great traders of the Mediterranean. During this time also, changes took place in the life of the cities. Troubles arose as some men became rich and others poor. The citizens tried to cure the ills of the state by changing the form of their government, until at last they reached a form in which, as nearly as possible, the people themselves decided all questions relating to the rule of the city. Democracy, as this is called, had never been tried before ; kings or nobles had commanded and people had obeyed. In Athens and other Greek cities democracy was successful, and many people ever since have believed it to be the best possible form of government. In some countries, our own among them, it is still in use.

The city of Athens grew up round a rock, the Acropolis or citadel, on which was the temple of the

goddess Athena. Surrounding the city was the territory of Attica. The farmers who dwelt there were
citizens of Athens, just as much as the people who
lived within the walls. Cornfields and vineyards lay
around the city, and the grey-green leaves of the
olive trees formed, as Euripides, an Athenian poet,
said, " a soft grey crown for a city beloved ". Farther
off were the hills, where goats grazed and bees
gathered the honey for which Athens soon became
famous. Five miles to the west was the harbour. In
the city's early days it was in the bay of Phalerum,
but after the Persian Wars it was removed to the
more protected inlet of Peiraeus.

In the seventh century B.C. there was much discontent among the Athenians. Some citizens had
large estates, while others had none at all, for they
had fallen into debt and had sold their land to pay
their debts. Many men had become slaves, for if a
man could not pay in any other way, he had to sell
himself to his creditor. There were no written laws
to which people could appeal in order to get justice.
The rulers of the city said what the law was, and
often they favoured the rich at the expense of the
poor. Things grew so bad that the many poor people
threatened to rebel against the few rich who governed
the city.

In 594 B.C. a noble called Solon tried to improve
matters. First of all he drew up a code of laws, and
had it engraved on stone pillars, which were set up

The Acropolis

in the market-place in Athens. All the citizens, nobles as well as poor people, had to obey these laws. Next Solon tried to help the poor. He made every Athenian citizen free once more by cancelling the debts which had forced men into slavery, and he said that no citizen could, in future, hold more than a certain amount of land. He thought, too, that if he encouraged trade there would be more work for people to do. So he started the export of olive oil, and this led to the making of big pottery jars to hold it. Thus Solon began the two industries which brought Athens great wealth in later days.

Solon made some changes in the government of Athens. He set up a new council of four hundred members, in which all except the poorest citizens could have a place, whereas in the old council, called the Areopagus, only men of noble birth could sit. He established a court in which cases of wrong-doing were tried by a jury of citizens. This was the first time that such an idea was put into practice, and to-day it is the custom of all civilized countries.

Solon's desire was to make Athens a place where every citizen could live comfortably and where justice would be the same for everyone. He says in one of his poems (for he was a poet as well as a statesman) :

> I wrote just laws and clear,
> Equal for base and good, that all might hear
> And find the path of Justice straight and plain.

But he did not succeed completely, for he still left too much power to the nobles. After a time Athens went back to her old ways. Then the poorer farmers rose against the nobles and set up a tyrant called Peisistratus. Tyrant in Greek simply meant a ruler who had complete power; it did not mean, as we take it to mean to-day, a cruel and oppressive person. Peisistratus, who was tyrant in Athens for nineteen years, was a good ruler. He followed Solon's example and did justice equally between rich and poor. To gain food for the increasing population in the city, he began trade with the Black Sea, on the shores of which were the wide cornlands that Greece lacked. To pay for the fountains and temples that he built to beautify the city, he worked gold mines in Thrace, and silver mines at Laureium, not far from Athens. He gave Athens a great religious festival of her own, the Panathenaea, and began the performance of plays in honour of the god Dionysus. All this helped to spread the renown of the city, and other cities began to look to her for advice and help if they were in trouble.

Peisistratus died in 527 B.C. His two sons followed him as rulers, but they were not as wise as their father. After some years, one was murdered and the other had to flee from Athens, and then the city went back to a democratic form of government. Led by Cleisthenes, the citizens arranged things in such a way that this time they really managed their own affairs. Every citizen could attend the assembly of the people and discuss the affairs of the city. A new Council of Five Hundred, chosen by the people themselves, was set up. As it was too big to sit all together, it was divided into groups or committees of fifty, each managing affairs for one-tenth of the year. The archons, the officers who carried out the orders of the council, were chosen from among the citizens by lot, and the people voted for ten generals to form a board to manage the army and to lead it in battle. In this way the people had a voice in everything that had to do with the welfare of the city, and since Cleisthenes kept the jury courts which Solon had set up, they also helped to do justice. Thus Athens became the best example which we have of a truly democratic community.

The rival of Athens for the first place among the Greek cities was Sparta. It was built twenty-five miles from the sea, on the banks of the Eurotas, in the valley of Laconia. Only those who dwelt in and around the city were citizens ; the inhabitants of the valley had no voice in the management of Spartan affairs. Sparta also ruled over the neighbouring land of Messenia, which she had conquered in the eighth century B.C. When this happened, the Messenians lost their freedom and became the slaves of their Spartan masters. But in the seventh century they rebelled. They were so nearly successful that the Spartans became afraid of them, and set themselves

The vale of Sparta

to become, above everything else, good soldiers, so that they would never be in such danger again.

At the age of seven a Spartan boy was taken from his home and placed in a school, where he remained till he was sixteen. Most of his time was spent in making his body strong. Drill and games, marching and climbing among the hills, filled his days. He had to bathe in the icy waters of the Eurotas, to wear only a single cloak, to eat coarse and scanty food, and to sleep on a hard straw mattress. His school building was of the simplest kind, with bare whitewashed walls, earthen floors, and rough wooden tables and benches. He was taught to admire courage and endurance as the greatest virtues, and trained in cunning, lying, and ruthlessness, for these might help him in warfare. Above all, he learned that he must give up his own pleasures to serve his city. He knew little of poetry and was not particularly interested in reading and writing. In music he was allowed to hear only stirring marching tunes that would direct his thoughts to warfare and heroism in battle.

Girls, though they were not taken away from home, were educated in much the same way. They, too, were taught to run and jump, to bear pain cheerfully, and to live simply and hardily, for they were to be the mothers of Spartan soldiers. So Spartan boys and girls, though they grew up healthy and beautiful, excelling at sports and full of love for their city, had little of the sense of freedom, the delight in poetry and art, and the desire for knowledge of the Athenians.

When a Spartan youth grew to manhood, he had to spend all his time training himself for warfare.

Spartan soldiers

He could not work for himself and his family, either as farmer or trader. He could only occasionally visit the house where his wife and children lived. He lived in a barrack with young men of his own age, giving from his estate his share of the food that was served, for young and old alike, at long tables in a public hall. "There were fifteen persons to a table or a few more or less ; each of them was obliged to bring in monthly a bushel of meal, eight gallons of wine, five pounds of cheese, two pounds and a half of figs, and a little money to buy flesh and fish. . . . The dish that was in highest esteem among them was black broth. The old men were so fond of it that they ranged themselves on one side to eat it, leaving the meat to the young people."

When a man was thirty, he became a member of the Assembly. At its meetings he gave his consent to the plans of the Council of Elders who managed the city's affairs, and helped to choose, once a year, the five ephors, whose business it was to watch over the city and see that the laws were strictly obeyed. Not until he was sixty could a Spartan become one of the twenty-eight members of the Council. If he was chosen for this, he became one of the most important citizens, for the Elders were the most powerful people in the city.

Sparta differed from all the other Greek cities in that she had kings throughout her whole history. There were always two of them, one from each of the two noblest families of Sparta. Their chief work was to lead the army in time of war and to act as high priests at great religious festivals. The kings were held in great honour among the citizens, but they lived as simply as everybody else, and had to obey the laws just like ordinary citizens. If they did wrong, they could be punished by the ephors.

The training of the Spartans made them the finest soldiers in Greece, famous everywhere for their bravery and endurance. But it also had bad effects. It led them to despise weakness and to care little for those who were ill and unhappy. It made them underhanded too ; if they could not win by fair means, they resorted to trickery. It kept them ignorant and prevented them from learning about the world, as other Greeks did through trade and sea-faring. They did not care for beautiful things, nor did they love poetry and plays. Because knowledge and love of the good and beautiful make men leaders much more than mere fighting power, the Spartans were never looked up to as the Athenians were ; and when the Persians set out to conquer the Greeks, it was Athens, not Sparta, that saved Hellas.

CHAPTER XVIII

The coming of the Persians

Herodotus tells how the Persians invaded Greece. The Athenians defeated the Persian army at Marathon. Leonidas and his Spartans fought to the death at Thermopylae.

The King with half the East at heel is marched
    from lands of morning ;
Their fighters drink the rivers up, their shafts
    benight the air.

UNTIL the Persians invaded their land, the Greeks had little experience of warfare against a powerful enemy. Sometimes they fought among themselves ; for instance, Athens in the time of Solon went to war with Megara for the possession of Salamis, their island neighbour. But they were not, like the Assyrians, a warrior people; they were chiefly interested in increasing the beauty of their cities and in expanding their trade. At the beginning of the fifth century they had to turn their thoughts to fighting in grim earnest. They were threatened with invasion by Darius, king of Persia, who was seeking to add more lands to his empire ; and if they were conquered, they would lose the freedom they valued so highly.

The story of the Persian Wars has been told by Herodotus, who was born while the struggle was going on. He says at the beginning of his book that he is writing it in order that "the great and wonderful deeds both of the Greeks and the barbarians may not pass unglorified".

Among the people whom Cyrus the Great conquered, when he built up the Persian Empire, were

Greeks in battle

the Ionian Greeks. Though they were left free to manage their own affairs, and only made to pay tribute and provide ships for the fleet, they felt they were despised by their countrymen across the sea for submitting to Persian rule. So in the reign of Darius they rebelled. Herodotus tells us how they sent an ambassador to Sparta to ask for help, and how the Spartans refused it, because they feared they would have to leave the coast and march inland through the wild country of Asia Minor. The ambassador went on to Athens, who promised them twenty ships to help them. Athens kept her promise, but the Ionian cities were beaten. And now it was the turn of the Athenians, for Darius was determined to punish the city that had helped the rebels.

The Athenians, whose soldiers were few in numbers compared with the Persian army, sent a swift runner to Sparta to ask for help. The Spartans answered that they were celebrating a religious festival, and could not come till the full moon was past. But the Persians were already besieging Eretria and had sent a large force to Marathon, ready to march on Athens. The city was defenceless, for her old walls had been destroyed. So the Athenian army, which was going to the help of Eretria, turned aside to Marathon ; and there, with the help of a thousand men from the little city of Plataea, they faced the enemy. Their courage was great, for " until this time the very name of Persian had been a terror to the Greeks ".

For several days the armies waited ; then the Greeks attacked. Trusting to their bronze armour, their shields and long spears, they " hurled themselves on them (the Persians) in a compact mass and fought with extraordinary courage ". It seemed at one time as if they must be defeated, for the picked Persian troops in the centre were too much for the thin Greek line. But on the wings the Greeks drove back their opponents, and then, turning round, they came to the rescue of the centre. The Persians were driven back to their ships. Seven of these were destroyed ; the rest set sail for Athens, hoping to reach it before the Athenian army. But they were too late. The Athenians were already there, and so they sailed away.

The Spartans came to Marathon. They saw the corpses of the Persians and the great mound under which lay the Athenian dead, and they went away praising the high deeds of the Athenians.

For a time Athens was saved. But the leaders of the Greeks knew well enough that the Persians would come again, and how were they to be met? Themistocles, one of the cleverest of the Athenians, urged that a fleet must be built, and that the Persians must be fought by sea as well as on land. Many people opposed Themistocles, for they did not realize that, as long as the Persian king could send his soldiers by sea, and land them anywhere in Greece, the city states would never be safe from attack. But Themistocles had his way. The Athenians made docks at Peiraeus ; they trained sailors and built a fleet of two hundred triremes. When, ten years later, the Persians came again, they found the Greeks ready to meet them on the sea.

Xerxes was now the " great king ". In 480 B.C. he set out from Sardis, the chief city of Lydia. Herodotus tells us of his army, of the baggage and the pack animals, of the soldiery drawn from forty-six nations, of the finely equipped Persian cavalry and infantry that formed the king's bodyguard. This great host crossed the Hellespont by two bridges of boats, and then marched through Thrace, Macedonia,

A Persian archer

and Thessaly, while the fleet sailed level with it along the coast. At Thermopylae, a narrow pass between the mountains and the sea, the Persians found the Greek army waiting for them. In it there were only three hundred Spartans, for, as before, the Spartan Elders had found an excuse for not sending the whole of their forces. But small though his band was, the

I   K

command was given to the Spartan king, Leonidas. All the other Greeks were well content to fight under his leadership.

Xerxes thought that, when the Greeks saw the size of his army, they would run away, but his spies told him they were quite undismayed. So after waiting four days, he ordered his men to attack. Owing to the narrowness of the pass, the Persians could gain no advantage from their numbers. Twice Xerxes sent his finest soldiers, the " Immortals ", against the Greeks, and twice they were beaten back. Then Xerxes tried another way. He learned through the treachery of a Greek, Ephialtes, that there was a pass through the mountains which led down into the plain behind the Greeks. In the dead of night he sent the Immortals up this path. Owing to a mistake, the Phocian soldiers set to guard it withdrew, leaving the way open for the Persians.

At daybreak the Greeks heard the news that a body of the enemy was coming down the mountain-side. Leonidas gathered his army together, and said that those who wished might go while there was yet time, but that he and his Spartans would fight to the end. The Thespians and the Thebans stayed ; the rest departed. Attacked both in front and behind, the Greeks fought desperately. In the middle of the battle Leonidas fell. Over his body a fierce struggle arose, "in which the Greeks four times drove back the enemy and at last by their great bravery succeeded in bearing off the body ". They withdrew to a hillock, and there they made their last stand, fighting till not a single man was left alive. On the hillock a stone lion was set up in honour of Leonidas. A memorial was afterwards erected to the Spartan soldiers, which bore this simple sentence: "Stranger, bear word to the Spartans that we lie here obedient to their charge ".

While the soldiers were fighting on land, the fleet, composed chiefly of Athenian ships, was holding the sea. The Persians found it impossible to turn out the Greeks from their position at Artemisium. Their cumbersome slow-moving vessels were no match for the swift Greek galleys, and they suffered greatly from storms which swept the rocky headlands of Euboea. But when the land way was open, it was useless for the fleet to fight any longer. The admiral gave orders to return to Peiraeus, where the people had already heard the news that Xerxes was marching on Athens. There was no hope of defence against such a host. The women and children were sent to the islands of Salamis and Aegina, and the men took to the ships. Athens was sacked and burned by the barbarians.

CHAPTER XIX

The defeat of the Persians

Greek and Persian ships fought at Salamis. The Greeks won the battle of Plataea. Xerxes gave up the attempt to conquer the Greeks.

ALL now depended on the fleet, but it was not easy to decide upon the best thing to do. The Athenians wished to stay in the bay of Salamis to defend Attica and the islands, where their wives and children were. But the other Greeks wanted to fall back to the coast of the Peloponnesus, where the Spartan army was still in readiness to defend the cities and the great wall which was being hastily built across the Isthmus. Themistocles led the party who wanted to fight at Salamis ; for he saw that, if once the fleet left the protected bay, it would be overcome by the greater numbers of the Persian ships. In spite of the wisdom of his argument, he was in danger of being overcome by the party for withdrawal ; so he sent one of his slaves secretly to the Persians, telling them that the Greeks were proposing to leave the bay. The Persian fleet sailed at once to meet them. Thus they found themselves face to face with the enemy's ships and had to fight.

The narrow strait, in which the Greek ships were gathered, was guarded on the one side by the coast of Attica, on the other by that of Salamis. As at Thermopylae, this meant that the Persians could gain no advantage from their large numbers. But the result of the battle was very different, for this time the

Greek war-galleys

Persians could not fall upon the rear of the Greeks. It was a straight fight between the Greeks in the bay and the Persians sailing up against them.

Now the foresight of Themistocles and the hard work of the Athenian shipbuilders were justified. The Persians advanced to the attack. The ships ran alongside one another, and Greeks and Persians came together in hand-to-hand fighting. Many were slain ; many fell overboard in the desperate struggle, or went down with the sinking ships. The seafaring Greeks easily swam ashore, but many of the Persians could not swim, and so were drowned. " Never in one day ", says Aeschylus, " died such a host, such tale untold of men." When the fleeing Persians were thrust back upon their own vessels, defeat was certain ; for in their confusion and entanglement they were at the mercy of the Greeks.

Aeschylus, who wrote a play called *The Persians*, puts this description of the battle into the mouth of a messenger to the Persian court :

> And first
> One Grecian bark plunged straight, and sheared away
> Bowsprit and stem of a Phoenician ship.
> And then each galley on some other's prow
> Came crashing in. Awhile our stream of ships
> Held onward, till within the narrowing creek
> Our jostling vessels were together driven,
> And none could aid another ; each on each
> Drave hard their brazen beaks, or brake away
> The oar-banks of each other, stem to stern,
> While the Greek galleys, with no lack of skill,
> Hemmed them and battered in their sides, and soon
> The hulls rolled over and the sea was hid
> Crowded with wrecks and butchery of men.
> No beach nor reef but was with corpses strewn,
> And every keel of our barbarian host
> Hurried to flee, in utter disarray.

After this disaster to his fleet, Xerxes decided to return to Asia at once. He left an able Persian general to continue the war. The Greeks had a respite during the winter, for armies only fought in summer in ancient times ; but the next year they had to take up the struggle again. In spite of the disaster to their city and the losses they had endured, the Athenians proudly refused an offer of terms. They gave answer to the Persian messenger : " As long as the sun keeps his present course, we will never join alliance with Xerxes. Nay, we shall oppose him unceasingly." Once more they pleaded with Sparta to help them save the Greeks. This time, though after a great deal of delay, the Spartans sent a large body of troops to join the Athenians and Plataeans in a last fight for Greek freedom.

The armies met near Plataea. The battle was fiercely fought, for the cavalry of the Persians gave them a great advantage over the Greeks ; and, says Herodotus, " in boldness and warlike spirit the Persians were not a whit inferior to the Greeks ". But Spartan courage and discipline carried the day. Though many were killed, the rest fought on until the Persians were driven back. The Athenians, too, played their part nobly. Simonides, a Greek poet, wrote beautiful epitaphs on both the Spartans and the Athenians who fell at Plataea. Here is the one he wrote for the Athenians :

> If the best merit be to lose life well,
> To us beyond all else that fortune came :
> In war, to give Greece liberty, we fell,
> Heirs of all time's imperishable fame.

What was left of Xerxes' great host went back to Asia, and the Persians never set foot in Greece again. Soon afterwards a Greek fleet, which had sailed across the Aegean, fell in with a new Persian fleet off Cape Mycale. The Persians, remembering Salamis, drew their ships up on the shore and prepared to fight on land. The Greeks won the battle and then burnt the ships.

All the Greek cities had suffered during the war, but Athens most of all. Her young men had been killed, her treasury was empty, her temples were in ruins and her homes destroyed. But she had won high honour, and the smaller states looked upon her as their saviour. Beside her stood Sparta, whose renown after Thermopylae and Plataea made many look to her as their future leader. For the Greeks had only driven back the Persians, they had not destroyed them. So long as the Persian Empire remained in being, there was danger of another invasion, and their hope lay in uniting under the leadership of one city. Athens or Sparta—which was it to be?

CHAPTER XX

The Delian League and the Athenian Empire

Athens made a league of cities. Pericles became leader in Athens. The Delian League was turned into the Athenian Empire.

AFTER the battle of Mycale, the Ionian Greeks rebelled against their Persian rulers. Thucydides, who takes up the story of Greece where Herodotus leaves it, says that they " grouped themselves into two parties, one round the Athenians and one round the Lacedaemonians. For these two states had been shown to be the most powerful ; the strength of the one was on the land, that of the other in her ships." The party that looked to Sparta soon found out its mistake. The first thought of the Spartans was to go home, " for it seemed to them a thing impossible that they should ever be on the watch to guard and protect Ionia ". They thought it more important to keep their position as the chief city in the Peloponnesus than to help their fellow Greeks to freedom. So they withdrew their ships from the fleet and their soldiers from Asia, and went back to Greece to look after their own affairs. Then the Ionian Greeks turned once again to Athens for help.

In spite of her misfortunes Athens was ready. Even while the Athenians, men, women, and children, were rebuilding their city and surrounding it with a great wall, built so hastily that, as Thucydides says, " the foundations are laid of stones of all kinds, and in some places not wrought or fitted, but placed just in the order they were brought by the different hands ", Themistocles was planning how he might help the Ionians. His scheme was to build up a league of states which would include the Ionian cities and the islands of the Aegean Sea. This league was to possess a fleet, which should police the sea and prevent the Persians from returning for another attack. Each state was to provide either ships or money, according to its size. Since Athens was the leader, she was to provide the admiral of the fleet.

The other cities agreed to this plan, and the Delian League was formed. The money collected was placed for safety in Apollo's shrine on the island of Delos, in the middle of the Aegean Sea. Much money flowed into the League's treasury. Before long only Athens and three large islands, Chios, Lesbos, and Samos, provided ships ; with the money contributed by the others, Athens built ships in the dockyard at Peiraeus. At Delos, too, was held a Council, which discussed with the Athenian leaders the plans of the League. Each state, whatever its size, sent one member ; by this means, it was intended that all states should have an equal voice in the management of affairs. This

A prize given at the Panathenaic Festival

League reminds us of the League of Nations, which has its meeting-place at Geneva, where all the member nations send their representatives to the Assembly, and to whose expenses all members contribute according to their means. But the aims of the two Leagues are different; for the League of Nations seeks to prevent war and to persuade people to give up armies, navies, and air forces, whereas the Delian League was formed to provide a large fleet, which might be used not only to protect the Greeks, but also to attack the Persians, if a suitable chance arose.

The first admiral of the fleet was Cimon, whose father, Miltiades, had led the Greeks at Marathon. Under his leadership the League fleet defeated a large Persian force at the mouth of the river Eurymedon. Then some leading Athenians, who disliked Cimon because he advised friendship with Sparta, persuaded the people to ostracize him, that is, to vote for his exile from the city. Ostracism was often used in Greek cities. It was one of the bad points in Greek democracy, for it weakened a city by depriving it of a leader when he was most needed. Athens was weakened by the ostracism of Cimon, and for a time the Persians gained the advantage. Then Athens regained her supremacy, and in 449 B.C. peace was made. The Persians promised not to bring their ships into the Aegean Sea or their troops to the lands around it. For forty years they kept their promise.

After Cimon was ostracized, Pericles became the leader in Athens. For fifteen years in succession he was elected by the people to the board of ten generals, set up by Cleisthenes. He belonged by birth to one of the oldest noble families in Athens, but he believed thoroughly in democracy. Even those who disagreed with him admired him as a good and upright man. Plutarch, who lived five hundred years later and wrote the lives of many Greek and Roman statesmen, praises his dignity and gentleness, and says : " The reason for his success was . . . the reputation of his life, and the confidence reposed in him as one who was manifestly proven to be utterly disinterested and superior to bribes."

Under the leadership of Pericles there was no bitter quarrel among the citizens and no ostracism, so the Athenians were able to devote all their energy to increasing the power of the city among the other city states of Greece. Pericles was what we should call to-day a great imperialist, that is, he believed that Athens should lead all the Greek states and direct their common action against any outside enemy, while each state remained free to manage its own affairs within its own walls. He set out to bring the mainland states into alliance with Athens, and for a time he was successful. Then Corinth grew afraid that Athens would interfere with her trade in the west, and, with the support of Sparta, she succeeded in breaking up the Athenian alliance.

Pericles also sought to increase the power of Athens in the Delian League. The plan of Themistocles, by which all members of the League were to be equal, had already been changed to one in which Athens was to be the leader, and the others were to follow her lead. Under Pericles the treasury of the League was moved to Athens, and the money was sometimes used for the benefit of Athens, instead of for the whole League. If a member of the League did not wish to do what Athens advised, the fleet was sent against her to force her to agree ; and if a city revolted against Athenian domination, her independence was taken away from her. Gradually the Delian League was turned into the Athenian Empire. One after another the members were made subject states, and their contribution to the treasury of the League became a tribute paid to the Athenian treasury. By the time peace was made with Persia, only the three big islands, Chios, Lesbos, and Samos, remained independent.

Athens did not treat her subjects badly. She gave them peace, put down piracy, and increased their trade. She encouraged them to set up a democratic government and law courts like her own, to visit Athens, especially at the Panathenaic Festival, and to feel proud of their connection with " the bulwark of Hellas ". But in spite of all this, they grew more and more to dislike her rule. The smaller cities found it difficult to pay the tribute. Many people thought the old aristocratic government better than the new Athenian democracy. All alike hated the garrisons of Athenian citizens settled in their midst, for these were a reminder that they were no longer free. This was where Athens' fault lay. She, who was proud of her own freedom, was now taking away freedom from her fellow Greeks. This brought its own punishment. When the struggle with Sparta came to a head, most of the old League cities deserted Athens ; and without their help, she was vanquished by the superior power of Sparta and her allies.

CHAPTER XXI

The Athenians at home

Pericles made Athens a beautiful city. The citizens prospered through trade and industry. They spent their money for the good of the city. Athenian women stayed at home and managed their households. Boys and men spent much time in the gymnasium.

An old man, comparing Athens in 431 B.C. with the city of his youth, would find its outward appearance very different. Both the city and the harbour were now encircled with stout stone walls, and long walls, built by Pericles, protected the five miles of road between the two. On the Acropolis was the Parthenon, the new temple of Athena. A fine gateway to the Acropolis, the Propylaea, had just been completed; and on an outstanding spur of rock outside the Propylaea stood the little temple of Nike, the goddess of victory. On the slope of the Acropolis was the theatre of Dionysus with its circular tiers of seats, its orchestra where the chorus in a play sang and danced, and its stage for the actors. Round the Agora (market-place) were dignified public buildings, the Council Chamber, the Hall of the King-Archon, and the fine painted portico, in which people met for business and talk. On all these buildings much money had been spent. The Parthenon and the Propylaea were built of white marble from Mount Pentelicus, and the best architects, sculptors, and painters in Greece were employed for their design and ornamentation. In the dignity and beauty of its public

buildings the Athens of Pericles was a city of which its inhabitants could feel justly proud.

Other parts of the city our old man would find more like that of his boyhood. The Athenians were in such a hurry to rebuild their city that they did not wait to replan it; they simply ran up their houses on the old sites. So the streets were winding and narrow, and the houses were huddled together and lightly built of brick and plaster. The houses of the richer citizens differed only in size from those of the poorer

ones, not in solidity or luxury. This was partly because many of the wealthiest people lived in country
houses on their estates outside the city, as wealthy
men do to-day, and partly because a rich Athenian
spent his money, not on his own comfort, but on his
city, providing a trireme for the fleet or organizing
public games and festivals. Even the better-class
Athenian houses were of a simple type, built round
a courtyard with a portico on one side. Furniture
was equally simple ; but, because the Athenians loved
beauty, even their chairs and small tables, their beds
and couches were made with graceful lines.

An Athenian gentleman, even if he lived in his
country house, spent much of his time in the streets
and public places of the city. After his household
business was despatched, he would go to the Agora,
where he would find friends with whom he could discuss the news, argue about the policy of Pericles, or
listen to one of the many orators who gathered round
them the idlers of the market-place. If he held a
public office, some of his time would have to be spent
in the Council House or, if it was his turn to serve
on the jury, in the law courts. If he had business
interests (and many Athenian gentlemen put their
money into trading ventures), he might have to go
down to Peiraeus to see the captain of his ship, to do
business with the bankers whose offices were on the
quays, or to arrange for the disposal of the goods
which he had obtained from his trading ventures.

After a simple midday meal of bread and cheese, fruit and wine, the well-to-do Athenian went to the gymnasium. Here he might wrestle and run and practise disc-throwing, or take part in a game similar to hockey. Before exercising, he stripped and oiled

Cutting up a fish for a banquet

his body carefully all over ; after his exercise was finished, he scraped away the oil, dust, and dirt with a bronze scraper, and washed himself thoroughly at the big stone basin in the hall or pavilion. Then he strolled out to watch others exercising, or joined a group of older men sitting under the porticoes. His evening would probably be spent at a banquet, for this provided another opportunity for the talk in which the Athenians delighted.

A dinner-party in Athens lasted a long time. When the guest reached the house, a slave took his sandals and washed his feet. Then he took his place on a cushioned couch with another guest. The food, which was served on small tables beside the couches, was chiefly fish, game, and vegetables, honey-cakes and fruit. Wine was mixed with water in a large two-handled jar, and served to the guests in shallow bowls of painted pottery. After the dinner was over, there were entertainments, given by actors and acrobats, flute-girls and singers.

Poorer citizens had not the same leisure for exercise and entertainment. If they were farmers, they were busy ploughing, sowing, and reaping, gathering the grapes and the olives, and bringing their produce to the market-place for sale. If they were craftsmen or shopkeepers, they had to look after their business in their homes or their little open shops. But even these spent some of their time on the affairs of the city, for any man who had a thriving business had slaves to help him. Every citizen attended the Assembly, when it met on the Pnyx. In order that even a poor man could take his turn of jury service and serve in the Council, if the lot fell on him, Pericles arranged that there should be a small payment for this work. Thus rich and poor met together in the service of the city. This kept alive a feeling of freedom and equality in Athens, and also provided the poor with some change from their work.

Women in Athens did not go out to dinner-parties
with their husbands or take any part in the affairs of
the city. They looked after their homes, and, if they
did not do this properly, their husbands sometimes
read them lectures. Xenophon tells us that Ischo-
machus said to his wife: "There is nothing, my dear,

Craftsmen at work

so useful or so beautiful in life as tidiness. How nice it
looks to see shoes neatly arranged in a row, and the
cloaks put away by themselves, the bedding too, and
the pots and pans and the table-linen and the china,
in fact everything looks better if neatly put away."

Women also spent much of their time in em-
broidery and in weaving material for clothing.
Greek women wore white or coloured linen dresses,

falling in soft folds from the shoulders to the feet. They were fastened on the shoulders with pins or brooches, and caught in at the waist with a girdle. Out of doors they wore a cloak over the dress, and

A lady's silver mirror

sometimes a large shady hat. Men wore a woollen tunic with, out of doors, a long piece of woollen material wrapped round them to form a cloak. An ordinary Athenian housewife did most of her weaving herself, but a rich lady had slaves to do it for her, as well as to do her shopping and to wait on her. Wealthy women in Athens had often very little to do, and spent their time in gossip or at their toilet. In the British Museum we can see some of the beautiful toilet articles and the finely made pins and brooches used by Athenian ladies.

An Athenian lady did not even have to look after her children herself. When they were small, they had a slave nurse. As soon as they were six, the boys went to school. There they learned to read, and to write on small wax tablets. Writing was not such a difficult task for them as for Sumerian or Egyptian boys, for the Greeks had an alphabet and put together their words with letters, as we do. Many of the Greek capital letters are like ours, though the small ones are, for the most part, formed differently. Other lessons were simple arithmetic, done with the help of a reckoning board, and the recitation of Homer's poems. Drill and sports occupied a good deal of time, and music was an important subject, for every educated Athenian was expected to sing and play the lyre or the flute. When he grew older, a boy might go with his father to the law courts and the market-place, where he would learn something of the law and the art of oratory. The Greeks thought much of the ability to speak well in public ; every Greek was trained in this art, and orators like Demosthenes were held in great respect.

Girls were not as fortunate as boys. What education they had was given them at home by a slave. It was not thought necessary to teach them to write or to read Homer, or, except in Sparta, to join in sports and gymnastics. Girls did not share their work and play with their brothers, as they do to-day, any more than women shared in public life with men.

CHAPTER XXII

Artists, poets, and thinkers in Greece

The Parthenon was the most beautiful temple in Greece. Pheidias made a wonderful statue of Athena for it. Athens was the home of poets as well as artists. Socrates was a citizen of Athens.

" WE are lovers of the beautiful ", said Pericles, "and we cultivate the mind." He was speaking for the Athenians, but his words apply to all the Greeks. In their love of beauty and their desire for freedom the Greeks differed markedly from the people of the Ancient East, and these two qualities are their greatest gifts to the world.

Though it is now in ruins, the Parthenon still shows something of its ancient beauty. It was raised on an oblong platform, reached by broad shallow steps. Its roof was supported on fluted columns, a single row at the sides and a double row at either end to form a portico. In the middle was the shrine of Athena, lighted by the sunshine that entered through the tall doorways at either end. The skill of Ictinus, its architect, is shown by the careful way in which each part of it was measured, so that the columns should appear equally far apart, the size of the lintel should be suited to the columns, and the pediment should be neither too high nor too low. This is what we mean when we speak of the perfect proportions of a Greek temple.

The pediments above the porticoes were filled with statues, and the outer wall of the shrine was also adorned with a band or frieze of sculpture. Both statues and frieze were the work of the sculptor, Pheidias, and his pupils. Parts of them are now in the British Museum. There we can see, pictured in marble, the procession to the Acropolis on Athena's festival day ; the priests and elders of the city, the maidens with the saffron-coloured robe they had woven to adorn the old wooden statue of the goddess, the knights on their prancing horses, the chariots of the wealthy Athenians, the victors in the games, musicians and bearers of offerings, and cows and sheep for the sacrifices. Pheidias also made a new statue of Athena to stand in the shrine, facing the eastern doorway. This statue, with its ivory head and arms, and its golden draperies, was thought to be one of the most beautiful in Greece ; its equal was the statue of Zeus in his temple at Olympia, also the work of Pheidias.

Pheidias is not the only Greek sculptor whose work is known to us. There was Myron, who made the beautiful disc-thrower ; Polycleitus, whose figure of a young man was so perfect that other sculptors took it as a model ; and the unknown artist who

The Parthenon as it is to-day

made the bronze charioteer that stood among the statues of victors at Delphi. There were numbers of sculptors who carved the tomb-stones of the Greeks with simple pictures, a mother with her baby, a young man with his favourite dog, or a little girl with her doll and her pet goose.

The Greeks liked to have beautiful things in their homes, as well as in their temples and public places. Statuettes in bronze and silver, and little pottery figures, showing women playing at knucklebones (a favourite game among the Greeks), or a slave nurse with a baby, ornamented their rooms. Their cups and plates, wine-jars and water-pots, were painted with pictures. Sometimes they were scenes from the poems of Homer or from legends like that of Demeter and Kore, and sometimes pictures of everyday life, such as pupils at school learning music, or a lady at her toilet. The Athenians were particularly skilful in painting pottery. Some of their finest vases were made to hold olive oil; for jars of oil were presented as prizes at the sports which formed part of the Pana-thenaic festival.

The Greeks were great poets as well as great artists. One of their earliest writers of poetry was a woman, Sappho. She wrote little songs that could be sung to the lyre :

> I have a little daughter rare
> That's like the golden flowers fair,
> My Cleis;

I would not take all Lydia wide,
No, nor lovely Greece beside
For Cleis.

The three poets whose works are best known to us are Aeschylus, Sophocles, and Euripides, all Athenians. It was the custom in Athens, in the time of Pericles, for the poets to write plays which were presented in the theatre below the Acropolis at the festival of Dionysus. Prizes were awarded to the plays which the judges pronounced the best. Aeschylus won the first prize thirteen times. The action of a Greek play was not unlike that of a modern one; but there was in addition a chorus which sang and danced at intervals during the progress of the play. It was for chorus-singing that the poets wrote some of their most beautiful poetry. This verse in praise of Athens is part of a song written by Sophocles in his play, *Oedipus at Colonus*:

For other glories, Athens dear,
Our mother city, praise to thee,
Glory of horses, prancing colts,
The ancient glory of the sea,
Gifts of the mighty god; for thou,
O Lord Poseidon, in this pride
Didst throne our city when we learned
First in our roads the horse to ride
With bit and bridle; thou didst teach
Our hands to ply the oar-blade fleet
Over the brine, swift following
The Fifty Sea-nymphs' dancing feet.

"Erect he rode on car that never reeled"

The greatest Greek plays are tragedies, that is, serious plays whose subjects are taken from the poems of Homer and the old legends. But the Greeks also enjoyed comedies, especially those of the Athenian, Aristophanes. Aristophanes wrote most of his plays during the Peloponnesian War, when Athens was no longer as peaceful and prosperous as she had been in the days of Pericles. He looked back to the good old times, and made fun of the way in which the Athenians quarrelled among themselves. He thought that Athenian boys were not being brought up as well as they used to be, and were losing their hardiness and their good manners. In one of his plays he gives a boy this advice :

> So come, my lad, be brave and choose
> The better part and me ;
> And you shall learn to hate hot baths
> And market-place and be
> Ashamed at all the shameful things,
> And rise to give your place
> To older people who come in,
> And keep from all disgrace,
> And Honour's badge try hard to wear,
> And always be polite
> At home, and never contradict
> Your father, wrong or right.

In the fifth century there were many men in Greece who sought to increase knowledge, and to teach people to think for themselves about good and bad conduct, whether it was in their own lives or in their actions as citizens. Most of these men were not Athenians by birth ; but, since Athens prized learning so highly, they came to the city and set up schools or gave public lectures in the Agora. Because they claimed to teach all knowledge, they are known as sophists, from the Greek word which means wisdom. Much of the teaching of the sophists was good, but some of it tended to make people think that their own lives were more important than the well-being of the city as a whole.

The greatest thinker of the time of Pericles, the stone-mason Socrates, was not, however, of this type. He taught that a good man and a good citizen were one and the same, and he tried to make people think for themselves what good conduct was. His way of teaching was by questioning people. He gathered around him a few young men, in the gymnasium or the market-place or the meadows outside the walls, and started a discussion. If his pupils gave him answers which showed they had not thought much about the matter they were discussing, he asked more questions, until at last he led them to see that opinions and conduct which are to be accounted good must be guided by reason, and not simply by custom or by what is most convenient. Socrates' teaching was so wise that we still go back to it as the basis for many of our rules of conduct. But the magistrates of Athens did not see this ; they thought that Socrates was leading the young men of the city to question the laws and to mock at the gods. They brought him to trial on a charge of impiety, and when he was found guilty, he was ordered to drink a cup of hemlock, a poison which would cause his death. His friends wanted to help him escape from prison; but he refused, for he had always taught that a citizen's first duty was obedience to the state.

That Athens, after the Persian Wars, was the home of the greatest artists and thinkers of Greece was largely due to the wise leadership of Pericles. He spent the wealth which Athens gained from her trade and her imperial position on buildings which called for the work of the finest artists. He encouraged private citizens to train choruses for the plays of the great poets, and provided opportunities for them to be seen in the city festivals. He invited to Athens the most learned men in Greece. The leisure which the Athenian citizen enjoyed gave him time to discuss freely with his fellows, and learning in those days was obtained far more by talking than by reading books. The renown which Athens gained under Pericles outlasted her wealth and power. We still look back to her as the home of beauty and freedom.

CHAPTER XXIII

How the city states destroyed one another

The city states of Greece fought among themselves. Sparta conquered Athens. Thebes conquered Sparta. Then the cities were conquered by Philip, king of Macedon.

THE free prosperous life of the Greek cities did not last. The rivalry between Athens and Sparta came to a head in 431 B.C., and in nearly a century of warfare, in which most of the city states joined on one side or the other, they were all so weakened that, when Philip, king of the neighbouring country of Macedon, invaded Greece, they were unable to stand against him.

The Peloponnesian War, as the first war between the city states is called, began in a trade quarrel between Corinth and Athens. Sparta came to the help of Corinth, and her example was followed by most of the other cities in the Peloponnesus and Boeotia. Beside her subject cities, the only important ally of Athens was Plataea. This meant that on land the Spartans and their allies were much stronger than the Athenians. But Athens had her navy, which was far better than any fleet which could be gathered

together by the Spartans. So, for the most part, the
Spartans were successful on land and the Athenians
won victories at sea.

In 429 misfortune befell Athens in the death of
Pericles, who had been among those that had fallen

ill of the plague which
ravaged the city a year
earlier. Bitter quarrels
then arose among the
Athenians. In every
city there were two
parties ; those who
wanted the govern-
ment of the city to be
in the hands of the
rich men only, and
those who believed that
all citizens should have
a share in the govern-
ment. In Athens
Pericles had been able
to unite these two
parties, and he had led them both in the imperial
policy which had brought the city her wealth and
power. But after his death there was no one in
Athens to take his place. Cleon, a leather-worker,
was the leader most favoured by the poorer citizens,
while the richer and more thoughtful ones supported Nicias, a well-to-do Athenian. But neither of

these men were statesmen like Pericles, and because of the quarrels in the city, Athens' strength for war was much weakened. Seeing this, some of the subject cities revolted, and part of the Athenian forces had to be used to suppress them. The severity with which such revolts were suppressed added greatly to the discontent of the subject cities, and this again weakened Athens in her efforts against Sparta.

In spite of these drawbacks, Athens held her own, and the war reached a point when neither side seemed likely to win and both were exhausted. So a peace was arranged by Nicias in 421. But the cities who had helped Sparta were not included in it. Corinth especially disliked this, and kept up her enmity to Athens.

Athens used the opportunity, which the peace brought her, to press on with her attempt to obtain more trade in the west, especially in Sicily. She fitted out a great expedition, sending both an army and a fleet, to attack Syracuse, the wealthiest and most powerful of the Greek cities in Sicily. This expedition was a terrible failure, chiefly because of the incompetence of Nicias, who was in supreme command. In the end, after a two years' siege, the Athenians were completely defeated, and their army was destroyed.

The failure of the expedition was a great disaster for Athens. She had spent much money on fitting out a fleet for it, and the finest and strongest of her young men had perished in the last fight. At home the failure increased the bitterness of the quarrels between leaders and parties. The Spartans at once took advantage of this to start the Peloponnesian War again. They invaded Attica and built a fort at Decelea. This prevented Athens from working the silver mines at Laureium which were among the chief sources of her wealth. Then Sparta did a thing which all truly patriotic Greeks condemned. She brought the Persians into the struggle, promising that she would help them to regain control of the Ionian cities, which had revolted against Athens, provided they supplied her with money to fit out a fleet. The Spartans decided to gather together a fleet because they saw that, so long as Athens could beat them on the sea, they could not hope to end the war, no matter how many victories they might gain on land. At first, as might be expected, they were not successful ; they needed time and experience to equal Athens in the art of naval warfare. And Athens, weakened though she was, made a tremendous effort to save her sea power and her subject cities. At Arginusae, near the island of Lesbos, the Athenians won a great victory over the Spartans, only to be completely defeated in the following year at the battle of Aegospotami in the Hellespont. The Athenian fleet had to surrender to the Spartan admiral, Lysander. Athens was besieged by land and sea, and finally was driven by famine to accept terms of peace.

This was in 404 B.C. Now it was Sparta's turn to dominate Greece. Though the Spartans left Athens free, in memory of what she had done for Greece in the past, they took from her all the cities which had belonged to her empire, and ruled them by Spartan officers, who tried to set up the system of rule by force that prevailed in Sparta. The cities found this rule much more oppressive than the Athenian democratic rule, and became even more discontented than they had been under Athens. In the Peloponnesus Sparta's allies were beginning to fear her power. The Greeks bore her a grudge for appealing to Persia for help, and for leaving the Ionian cities in Persian hands at the end of the war. Moreover, the Spartan alliance with Persia ended with the war, and soon Persia was in league with her enemies. The Athenian admiral who had been defeated at Aegospotami was placed in command of the Persian fleet, and the Athenians took Persian gold to pay for the rebuilding of the Long Walls, which had been destroyed by order of the Spartans. That even Athens should accept Persian help shows the bad effect on the cities of the party quarrels and the long warfare.

As a result of this, another war broke out in 371. Thebes, the chief of the Boeotian cities, now took the lead against Sparta, and she was aided by Corinth, Athens, Argos, and the Persian fleet. The Theban general, Epaminondas, who was a true patriot and wanted to free the Greeks from dependence on

Persia, defeated the Spartans at Leuctra, and invaded Spartan territory. Nine years later he won another great victory at Mantinea, which ended completely the power of Sparta.

But another enemy was at hand. Philip, king of Macedon, saw in the quarrels of the Greeks an opportunity to extend his kingdom. He invaded Greece. Without Epaminondas, who had been killed at Mantinea, the Thebans could not withstand him, and Athens, who had now regained some of her power, was slow to move. Demosthenes, the great Athenian orator, said :

> We Greeks see all this, and what do we do ? . . . So divided are we that up to this moment we have not been able to do a single thing to help ourselves. . . . We watch this fellow overshadowing Greece and yet, so far as I can see, each of us determines to profit by the time it takes Philip to destroy our neighbours instead of doing what we can to save our country.

Finally Athens agreed to help Thebes, but it was too late. Philip defeated the Greek army at Chaeronea, and the cities, except Sparta, fell under his rule.

Among all this warfare, it would seem as if the beauty, the love of poetry and the desire for knowledge, which had distinguished Athens in the fifth century, must disappear. One of the evils of war is that everybody is so occupied in thinking about destruction that there is no time or energy left for the beautiful things of life. But in spite of the strain

Demosthenes

of the long warfare, the Athenians still produced fine works of art and continued their quest for knowledge. During the Peloponnesian War another temple, the Erechtheum, was built on the Acropolis. In the fourth century Praxiteles made beautiful statues, such as the Hermes of Olympia. Lysippus modelled figures of athletes and made portrait busts of famous men, a form of sculpture hitherto little practised in Greece. The beautiful figure of Demeter in the British Museum was made in the same century.

The great writers of the fourth century were prose writers. Xenophon followed in the footsteps of Herodotus and Thucydides ; it is he who tells us of the march of the Ten Thousand Greeks, through the sands of Mesopotamia and the snow-covered mountains of Asia, until they reached their beloved blue sea again. Two great men wrote books which are still widely read to-day. Plato wrote down the teaching of his master, Socrates, in a book which he called *The Republic*, showing how a city could best be governed and how its citizens might live a good life. Aristotle, who was only a young man when Plato died, also wrote two books on the same subjects, the *Politics* and the *Ethics*. Thus war did not completely stop the Greeks from seeking knowledge.

CHAPTER XXIV

Alexander the Great and the Hellenistic world

Alexander the Great built up a wide empire. He founded the city of Alexandria in Egypt. He took Greek learning to the East. The learning of the Hellenistic world passed on to the Romans.

ALEXANDER OF MACEDON was only twenty years old when his father was murdered in 336 B.C. But, though young, he was well able to take up the rule of the kingdom which Philip had built up. He was handsome and a great athlete. He was a fine general, and endeared himself to his soldiers by his willingness to share hardships and dangers with them. His army was the best in the world, better even than that of the Persian king ; for Philip had spent much time and money on training his soldiers, and had introduced a new method of fighting, placing his men about a yard apart in slanting lines, and arming the rear ranks with longer spears than the front ranks. This was more effective than the straight closely packed lines in which bodies of soldiers had hitherto fought. Alexander had wealth too, for Philip had conquered the land in which were the famous gold mines of Mount Pangaeus, and had exacted tribute from the cities he conquered. His ambition was to become the greatest ruler in the world. For this he must conquer the Persian Empire; and, as soon as he became king, he began to make plans for this great enterprise.

But before he could invade Persia, he had to subdue a revolt of the Greek cities, which seized the opportunity of Philip's death to try to regain their freedom. They found Alexander every whit as ruthless as his father. Though he had a great love for the Greeks, having had Aristotle as his teacher in his boyhood, he was not prepared to give them freedom. He firmly suppressed the rebellion of the cities; Thebes was completely destroyed, except the house of the poet Pindar; Athens, however, was treated more leniently, because Alexander looked upon it as the home of Greek literature and Greek art. Then the king sought to bind the Greeks to him by gathering their finest soldiers into his army for the invasion of Persia.

It would take too long to follow Alexander in every step of his conquests. He marched through Asia, Syria, and Palestine to Egypt, winning two great battles on his way at the river Granicus and at Issus. Then he set out for Mesopotamia, and defeated the Persian king—another Darius—at Arbela. He became master of the cities of Babylon, Susa, and Persepolis, and King of the Persians, for Darius was killed by his own followers after the battle of Arbela.

Then he marched through the eastern provinces of the empire, enforcing obedience to his orders, crossed the mountain barrier of western India, and descended into the valley of the Indus. His plan was to reach the Ganges, thought then to be the edge of the world. But his soldiers were worn out; for eight years they had been marching and fighting without any rest, and they refused to follow him farther. He had perforce to march down the Indus valley to the sea, and thence to return to Susa.

There the king's presence was sorely needed. When Alexander had taken the title of Persian king, he had adopted many Persian customs. He held his court with Eastern splendour, he married a Persian princess, and gave the Persian nobles high places at court and in the army. In this way he sought to bring Greeks, Macedonians, and Persians together, so that in the end they might become one nation. But the Greeks and Macedonians despised the Persians as barbarians, and, while the king was away, there was much quarrelling between them and much misgovernment by the royal officers. Alexander restored order; then he began to prepare another expedition to conquer Arabia, the only part of the Eastern world still outside his empire. At Babylon he fell ill of a fever and in ten days he was dead. He was only thirty-three years old; he had been king only thirteen years; yet he had conquered nearly all the known world. His empire was larger than any

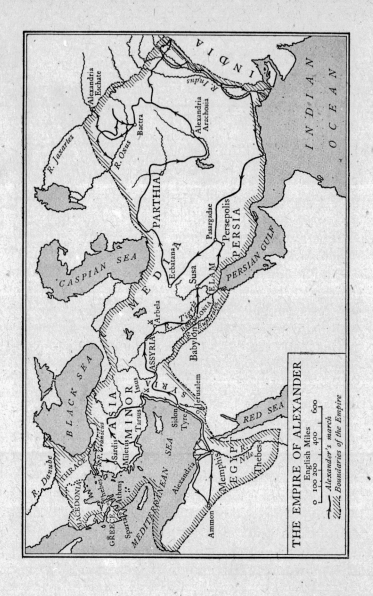

THE EMPIRE OF ALEXANDER

English Miles

0   100 200   400   600

→ Alexander's march
////// Boundaries of the Empire

empire of the Ancient East ; his renown as a conqueror spread even to the city of Rome, which was to build up the next great empire in history.

The people of the ancient world admired Alexander for his generalship, his victories and his wide conquests, for to them power and the rule over many lands seemed the test of a great monarch ; to-day we admire his efforts to bring order and progress to his subjects. His love of everything Greek made him desire to introduce the Greek ideas of life, Greek architecture and sculpture, Greek literature and learning among his Eastern subjects. Wherever he went, he built cities on the Greek model, first to be garrison towns, then to be centres for the spread of Greek culture. Of these cities Alexandria, at the mouth of the Nile, is still a flourishing town. In Roman times it was among the chief cities of the civilized world, famous for its library and its learned men. Though Alexander could not set up the Greek form of democratic government in the East (for the Eastern peoples were not yet educated enough to govern themselves), he tried to ensure that his governors in the provinces should rule justly. He organized trade routes and encouraged industry. If his work in these respects does not occupy such a large part in the history books as the story of his conquests, it is because he died before he had time to carry it out as he intended. After his death there was no one to keep his empire together. His generals divided the lands between them. Egypt became independent under its governor, Ptolemy; Asia was ruled by Seleucus; and Macedon and Greece fell into the hands of Cassander, his viceroy in Europe.

Alexander's work did not perish entirely. The people of the East continued to use the Greek customs which he had introduced, and to carry on the Greek learning, particularly in those subjects which to-day are included in the term science. To the Greeks the word science meant knowledge of every kind; in modern times it is more often used to mean subjects like astronomy, mathematics, botany, and medicine. In these subjects the Greeks had already made many discoveries. They had learned a great deal more than the Babylonians about the movements of the stars; they had discovered that the earth was round, and had made maps. They knew far more about mathematics than the ancient Egyptians. Aristotle had observed the ways of fish and insects, even of such a common thing as the house fly. Hippocrates had tried to find cures for many illnesses. The scholars of the Hellenistic world, as the lands which formed Alexander's empire are called, carried on the work of the Greeks. Euclid lived in these days and taught the system of geometry which bears his name, and the discoveries of Archimedes are known to every schoolboy who learns physics to-day. A scholar called Heron came near to discovering the steam engine. All these scholars had

" With outspread wings and draperies blown by the wind "

none of the modern devices for scientific study, such as the microscope and the telescope, but, in spite of this, they discovered many things about the world which are part of the learning of to-day.

The Hellenistic world had its artists also. Among these were the architects who built the lighthouse of Alexandria, one of the Seven Wonders of the World, and adorned the Acropolis at Pergamum in Asia Minor with colonnaded buildings and a sculptured altar to Zeus. Statues made by Hellenistic sculptors are to be seen in many museums to-day. Two beautiful ones are in the Louvre in Paris. One, which was found in the island of Melos, represents the goddess Aphrodite. The other is a marble figure of Victory, with outspread wings and draperies blown by the wind, which was set up at Samothrace in thanksgiving for a victory at sea.

The knowledge and art of the Hellenistic world is part of our heritage, together with that of the Greeks; for when the Romans became in their turn the conquerors of the world, they preserved it as part of their own art and learning, and through them it has come down to us.

CHAPTER XXV

The City of the Seven Hills

The city of Rome was on the banks of the Tiber. The Romans conquered all their neighbours and ruled the whole of Italy.

LORD BYRON, an English poet, described Italy as

<blockquote>
a land
Which was the mightiest in its old command
And is the loveliest.
</blockquote>

Nature made Italy beautiful : the Romans made her mighty. Their city, which, according to their own story, was founded by Romulus in 753 B.C., was at first so small that we should call it a village. In time it became the leading city in Italy, and then the capital of a great empire.

To-day the kingdom of Italy includes the wide plain, watered by the river Po, which lies between the Alps and the Apennines. The ancient Romans called this plain *Gallia Cisalpina*, that is, Gaul-this-side-of-the Alps. For them Italy was the peninsula jutting out into the Mediterranean Sea. Its backbone was the long southward ridge of the Apennines, and its fertile lands were the valleys and plains lying between the mountains and the western coast. The city of Rome grew up on the banks of the Tiber, the largest of the rivers which flowed through the western valleys.

The climate of Italy is a warm one, with rain enough to make the land fertile. Corn grows easily in the rich soil; grapes and olives ripen in the hot sunshine; and there is plenty of good pasture for cattle. Virgil, a Roman poet, said of Italy:

> But here abundant harvest fills
> The land. . . .
> Here dwells the spring, and summer-tide
> Tarries beyond her season due.
> Our cattle twice their breed renew.
> Two apple crops the trees provide.

Thousands of years ago, a stone-using people dwelt in this land. Then came immigrants using copper and bronze; after them came people who made use of iron as well. These iron-using immigrants were the Umbrians, who settled in the north and centre of the peninsula; the Latin tribes, who made their homes in the valley of the Tiber; and the Samnites, who occupied the southern hills and valleys. These people all came through the mountain passes of the Alps. Over the sea from Asia came the Etruscans, a warlike race, who pushed back the Umbrians into the mountains and occupied the land which lay to the north of the Tiber. Lastly, the Greeks founded their colonies on the south-western coast and in Sicily.

ROME AND
HER NEIGHBOURS

===== *Roads made during
wars of expansion*

Greek cities <u>underlined</u>

GAULS

ETRUSCANS

UMBRIANS

R. Rubicon

Narnia

CORSICA

Veii

Rome

Ostia

LATINS

APPIAN

Capua

Beneventum

WAY

Naples

Venusia

<u>Cumae</u>

<u>Paestum</u>

<u>Tarentum</u>

SARDINIA

<u>Sybaris</u>

<u>Croton</u>

<u>Rhegium</u>

S I C I L Y

Carthage

<u>Syracuse</u>

Both Etruscans and Greeks brought with them to Italy the civilization they had already attained in their own countries. Among other things, the Romans learned the art of writing from the Greeks and the use of the arch in building from the Etruscans.

The little city founded by Romulus grew gradually in size, until it included the six low hills around the Palatine Hill. This is why Rome is called the City of the Seven Hills. Like the early Greeks, the people soon became traders as well as farmers, exchanging their goods with Carthaginians, Greeks, and Etruscans. Trade brought them riches, but it also led to quarrels with their neighbours. Farmers and traders had then to put aside their business and serve in the Roman army, which was arranged in regiments of one hundred men, called centuries.

With the tribes who dwelt in the plain of Latium the Romans were at first friendly, for they were of the same race. They made a Latin League, of which Rome became the leader. But as time went on, the Latin cities became jealous of the Roman power. War broke out ; one by one the cities were conquered, and Rome became the ruler of Latium.

While this warfare was going on, the Romans had also to fight the Etruscans, who wanted to add the wealthy city on their borders to their own territories. There were many wars between Romans and Etruscans. Finally the Romans took the important Etruscan city of Veii, and by degrees extended their rule over the whole territory of the Etruscans.

More dangerous to Rome than either Latin or Etruscan enmity were the barbarian Gauls, who came down over the Apennines to plunder and burn the Roman farms. In 390 B.C. a large barbarian army captured and burned the city. But they could not take the Capitol, the fortified hill on which stood the temple of Jupiter and Juno. The Romans told a story of how this was saved by Juno's sacred geese. One dark night, a party of Gauls climbed the steep cliff that formed one side of the hill. They had almost reached the top, when the geese began to cackle loudly. This gave the alarm, and the Gauls

An Etruscan warrior

were driven back. They did not attempt to storm the Capitol again, and soon afterwards they were driven away by Camillus, a Roman general, who had already fought bravely against the Etruscans. The city was rebuilt, but the Romans had lost, among other things, all the records of their early history. Livy, who wrote the first history of Rome nearly four hundred years later, could only explain the beginnings of the city by stories like that of Romulus and Remus.

After they had conquered Latium, the Romans came into conflict with the people who lived in the mountains bordering the plain. The strongest of the mountain tribes were the Samnites, a brave and independent people. The Romans waged three wars against them before they finally subdued them. Then they went to war with the Greek cities, with whom they quarrelled over trade. Though the Greeks were helped by Pyrrhus, king of Epirus, a country lying to the north of Greece, they too had to submit. The Roman soldiers and the Roman people were so determined never to give in that they always won in the end. They were defeated many times during their wars, but they always gathered fresh armies and began to fight again. By 275 B.C. they ruled over the whole peninsula. It had taken over two hundred years for Rome to become mistress of Italy, and had cost the lives of many brave Romans.

CHAPTER XXVI

The Roman Republic

Kings ruled Rome in early times. Then the city became a republic. At first the patricians governed it. Then the plebeians gained a share in the government. The Romans made good roads in Italy.

WHILE the Romans were extending their rule, they were also learning how to govern themselves. For nearly two hundred and fifty years after the city was founded, it was ruled by kings. Some of these did much good for the people, building a wall round the city and a bridge over the river, temples for worship, a market-place for trade, and a big drain to carry off the water that ran down into the valleys between the hills. Others, however, were cruel and oppressive, and the seventh king, Tarquin the Proud, was so hated that in 509 B.C. he had to flee from the city. He was the last king in Rome.

Then Rome became a republic. Two consuls, who were chosen by the people, managed the affairs of the city and led the army in battle. They wore togas with a purple stripe, and when they went out in the city, they were accompanied by twelve lictors, who each carried a bundle of rods with an axe in the middle. This was a sign of the consuls' authority. They were helped by a council of wise men called the Senate, and sometimes the people met together in the Assembly to approve the decisions of the consuls and the Senate.

This sounds like a democracy, such as Athens was in the time of Pericles. But it was not really so. The citizens of Rome were divided into two classes, patricians and plebeians. The patricians were the nobles and the richer people ; the plebeians were the poorer farmers and the craftsmen. They could not sit in the Senate nor hold the office of consul, so that really they had little to do with the government of the city. Before Rome could be called a democracy, like the Greek cities, the plebeians had to gain equality with the patricians. It took them nearly one hundred and fifty years to do this.

The first thing the plebeians wanted was equal justice with the patricians, for sometimes, if a dispute arose between a patrician and a plebeian, the magistrate would favour the patrician. So they tried to get plebeian officers appointed who would look after their interests. After a struggle they succeeded ; two " tribunes of the people " were appointed to whom any plebeian could go for help if he felt he were being unjustly treated.

Next they gained something even more important than this. Until 450 B.C. the Roman law was known only to the magistrates or officials. The plebeians wanted it to be written, so that everybody might know it and be sure that judgment was given according to it. So, just as in Babylon and Athens the laws were written and set up in a public place, the law of Rome was written on bronze tablets and set up in the Forum, the market-place of Rome. The Twelve Tables of the Law were considered so important that boys had to learn them by heart.

The other things the plebeians wanted were to be able to sit in the Senate and to be elected magistrates. In the early days of the republic the only magistrates were the consuls, but they were often away from the city leading the army, and then there was nobody to look after affairs in Rome. So as time went on, other magistrates were appointed. Praetors were chosen to act as judges, quaestors to take care of the money which the citizens paid into the treasury, aediles to keep order, and censors to look after the public lands. All these, like the consuls, were at first patricians. By degrees, the plebeians gained the right to be elected lesser magistrates, and even to occupy the position of consul. The magistrates only held their office for a year ; after that they sat in the Senate. By becoming magistrates, the plebeians were also able to sit in the Senate, and at last there seemed to be real democracy in Rome.

As Rome conquered the people of Italy, she had to find out the best way of governing them. She chose a different method from that of the conquerors of

The oldest road leading out of Rome

earlier times. She did not take them away from their homes, as the Assyrian kings had done ; nor did she make slaves of them, as the Spartans did the Messenians. She tried to make them like her rule and feel proud to be her subjects. She let the Italian cities manage their own affairs, allowing them to appoint their magistrates and to have their own councils and assemblies. But they could not go to war or make alliances without her consent, and a Roman official was appointed in every city to see that justice was done according to Roman ideas.

The Italians were encouraged to think of themselves as part of the Roman state. Many of them were made Roman citizens. This meant that, though they still lived in their own city, they could go to Rome to help elect the magistrates and pass the laws in the Assembly, and if they were accused of wrong-doing, they could claim to be tried by Roman law. Those who were not given full citizenship were encouraged to trade with Rome and to marry Roman wives. Many Roman colonies were founded among the Italian cities, and Romans and Italians learned to live as neighbours.

Good roads made it easy for people to travel between Rome and their own cities. Though the Romans had no machines, such as pneumatic drills and steam-rollers, they dug out the soil and filled in the wide shallow trench with layers of strengthening materials as we do. On the rammed earth at the bottom they placed a bedding of cobble-stones, then a layer of rubble mixed with lime, and then a layer of fine concrete. On this they placed a surface of large paving-stones. The Roman road-makers did their work so well that their roads were used for hun-

An instrument for levelling a road

dreds of years, and traces of them can still be found in many places.

Cicero, who was born at Arpinum in the second century B.C., has told us what many Italians felt about Rome. He said, " I will never forget that Rome is my greater Fatherland, and that my native town is but a portion of Rome ". This pride in being part of the Roman state grew up in Italy because the Romans were so wise in their treatment of the people under their rule. One of the best things they left to the people who came after them was the example of how to rule others.

CHAPTER XXVII

A citizen of the Republic

The Roman was a good farmer. He directed the slaves who worked on the farm and all the household affairs. He looked after the worship of the household gods. He served in the army when necessary.

LET us see how an ordinary Roman citizen lived in the early years of the Republic. For convenience we will call him Gaius Fabius. Every Roman had at least two names, a personal name and the name of the large family or *gens* to which he belonged. In later times a third name was added.

To Gaius Fabius his home was an important place. He did not, like an Athenian, use it only for eating and sleeping. He was always ready to do his duty to his city, to fight for her and work for her. He was proud to be a Roman citizen. But his home, his family, and his household gods were the centre of his life.

The estate which belonged to Gaius Fabius lay in the farmlands surrounding the city. His home was a very simple one. It consisted of a large central room, called the *atrium*, with a few storerooms and bedrooms around it. The front door opened straight into the *atrium* ; in the middle was a shallow tank into which rain-water fell from a hole in the roof ; opposite the door was a hearth. Against one wall

was the chest in which Gaius kept his family treasures. In the *atrium* meals were cooked and eaten, and the children played, while their mother spun and wove and looked after her household. If Gaius Fabius had been a

A plough

poor man, the family would have slept there too. But Gaius was a patrician, and his house, though simple, was better than those of the poorer people.

Gaius Fabius was the most important person in the household. The whole family, which included his slaves as well as his wife and children, had to do exactly as he told them. He managed all the household affairs, as well as the work on his estate. His slaves did most of the actual work, but he directed everything. He saw that the fields were ploughed and the seed sown in spring. As the long summer waned he superintended the harvesting of the corn, the grapes, and the olives.

A farm-cart

He saw that the acorns were gathered for food for the pigs, and that the byres and the sheep-pens were repaired against the cold winds of winter. He arranged the winter work for the slaves, basket-making and wood-cutting and repairing the farming implements. Gaius Fabius, like most Romans, was a good farmer.

With all this work to do, he had not much time to saunter about the market-place talking about public affairs, like the Greeks. Nor did he spend his time in daily exercise, as the Greeks did. His chief work in life was to look after his land, manage his household, and bring up his sons to be brave and loyal citizens of Rome. His wife helped him in all these things, and when he had to leave his home and fight in the army, she directed the work of the household and the estate until he came back.

One of Gaius Fabius' chief duties was to look after the daily worship of the household gods. The Romans believed that all around them were spirit-gods, whose special work it was to care for the household and the farm. These gods could keep away evil and bring good fortune. But in return for this the whole household must pay them honour and give them offerings. In all their dealings the Romans believed in the importance of making an agreement and fulfilling it exactly. They thought that they had a bargain with the gods, who in return for protection were to be given worship. This worship had to be carefully carried out. If anything was left undone, misfortunes would befall the family, the crops would be blighted, and the cattle perish.

In the *atrium* of Gaius' house was a shrine where offerings of flowers, fruit, and wine were made. Every day began with prayers and an offering to the Lares and Penates, who looked after the welfare of the estate and the food of the household. At the chief meal of the day, Gaius placed some of the food on the hearth as an offering to the goddess Vesta, who watched over the fire which gave warmth to the household. He also made offerings to Janus, in whose care was the door of the house. Janus watched over the family, as they went out in the morning and came in again at night.

Beside the daily worship, there were special festivals of the family gods. In the spring Gaius Fabius gave all his slaves a holiday for the blessing of the fields. The images of the gods were carried in procession round the farm, while the children strewed flowers in front of them. Gaius offered sacrifices of cattle on an altar set up on the edge of his estate, and said a prayer, " that thou mayest suffer our crops, our corn, our vines and bushes to grow and come to prosperity ; that thou mayest preserve the shepherd and the flocks in safety and grant health and strength to me, to my home, and to my household ".

In the winter there was another festival, which took place in the house. The *atrium* was lighted up with oil-lamps and candles, and everybody played games and gave each other presents, as we do at Christmas.

The household gods were not the only ones that Gaius and his family worshipped. Like the Greeks, the Romans had gods who watched over the city as a whole. Jupiter and his wife Juno were, like Zeus and Hera, the chief of the gods. Minerva was the goddess of wisdom, like Athena. On festival days Gaius and his family went to the Capitoline Hill to worship them with the other citizens, and to be present when the priests offered the sacrifices. Sometimes Gaius went to the Campus Martius, where Mars, the god of war, had his temple. This was outside the city, for the Romans would not allow any-

thing connected with war to come within the walls. As he passed through the Forum, he would see the little round temple of Vesta, where priestesses, called the Vestal Virgins, looked after the fire on the city hearth. This fire was kept burning the whole year round, for just as the family would suffer if the fire on the family hearth went out, so the city would suffer if the fire on the city hearth did not burn constantly.

Reverence for the gods and the due carrying-out of the ceremonies of household worship were the chief things Gaius Fabius taught his sons. He taught them also obedience to the law, as well as to the mother and himself, for this was one of the things all Roman children had to learn very early. He also taught them reading and writing, but not much else. The Roman was not, like the Athenian, of a thoughtful nature. He did not often want to know the reason of things, nor did he love beautiful things as the Greeks did. He was a practical, hard-working farmer. If he had been asked what were the best things he had done in life, he might have answered with the words carved on the tombstone of an unknown Roman soldier, " I loved my friends, I kept my faith, and attended to my duties ".

CHAPTER XXVIII

Rome and Carthage

The Romans fought three wars with Carthage. Hannibal, a great soldier, was defeated. Carthage was destroyed. Rome became mistress of the Mediterranean.

IN the third century B.C. Carthage was a wealthy trading city. Its great double harbour was the pride of all its citizens. Beside the quays of the outer harbour, protected by its narrow entrance, lay their broad-built merchant ships ; in the round inner basin their warships were berthed. Beyond the harbour was the market-place with the temple of Apollo; near by were the shrines of Baal and Tanit, the old Phoenician gods. Narrow streets, overshadowed by high stone houses, led up to the citadel and the temple of Eshmun, the god of wealth and healing. Outside the massive walls of the city were the villas of the Carthaginian nobles, surrounded by orchards, vineyards, cornfields, and olive groves.

The outer harbour was the busiest place in the city, for the Carthaginians were the foremost traders of the western Mediterranean. Their colonies were dotted along the coasts of Africa and Spain. Sardinia and the greater part of Sicily belonged to them. Their ships were to be seen in all the Mediterranean ports, and far beyond the Pillars of Hercules. They fetched gold and ivory from Africa, silver from Spain and tin from Britain, exchanging for these corn, wine and oil, purple-dyed clóth, glass beads and coloured ribbons.

The eagerness of the Carthaginians to increase their trade made them many enemies. In their wars with the Greeks and Etruscans they were the victors, for they had a fine army and navy. Their quinque-remes, propelled by large oars that needed five men to pull them, protected the city and her outposts, and made the Carthaginians superior to any other sea-going people. Their army was composed of hired soldiers who made fighting their business: Numidian horsemen, slingers from the Balearic Islands, Spanish infantry, and archers mounted on elephants. These soldiers were well trained and equipped, but they had not the love of their city to inspire them to deeds of valour, like the Greek and Roman citizen armies.

While Rome was busy in Italy, she was on friendly terms with Carthage. But when she began to take an interest in things outside Italy, the two cities became enemies. The Carthaginians were afraid that Rome would interfere with their trade in the Mediter-ranean. Roman and Carthaginian sailors often quarrelled with one another when they met in the harbours, and this led to war.

The first of the Punic Wars, as they are called, began in 264 B.C. It was fought largely on the sea. The Romans set to work to build a fleet to equal that of the Carthaginians. One hundred and twenty war galleys were built in sixty days. Though the Romans were at first victorious, their hopes were shattered when their ships were destroyed in a hard-fought

battle off the coast of Sicily. With true Roman perseverance, they built a new fleet, even larger than the first, and continued the struggle. At last, after twenty-three years of warfare, the Carthaginians asked for peace. They had to pay a large sum in tribute and give up Sicily and Sardinia to Rome.

The next war began in 218 B.C. The Carthaginian army was led by Hannibal, whose father had hated Rome so much that he had made his little son swear, "I will never hold friendship with the Romans". Hannibal was only twenty-six when he set out to invade Italy. He had to march by land, for the Romans now held the sea. This meant crossing the Alps, which was so difficult a task that the Romans did not believe he could do it. The way lay through a pass thick with boulders and deep in mud. On one side, precipices fell sharply for hundreds of feet; on the other, barbarians lay in ambush in the hills to roll down large rocks on the long column of cavalry, infantry, elephants and baggage animals. It took nine days to reach the summit of the pass. The descent was even worse, for on the frozen ground the elephants could not keep their footing, and many men were killed as the unwieldy animals rolled down the steep slopes.

At last Hannibal reached the plain. The Romans hastily sent an army under the consul Publius Cornelius Scipio to oppose him. In spite of the weariness of his men, Hannibal at once attacked Scipio and completely defeated him. Next year he defeated and killed the consul Flaminius at the battle of Lake Trasimene, and then he won a third victory at Cannae.

Hannibal was a great soldier, but he could not win victories year after year without fresh forces and supplies; and the Carthaginians, who were more interested in their trade than in the war, refused to send reinforcements. Nor did the Italian allies of Rome, whom he hoped to win over to his side, give him much support. Though he remained in Italy for twelve years longer, he never gained another great victory. Once he reached the gates of Rome, but his forces were insufficient to take the city. At last he received orders from Carthage to return to Africa, for a Roman army, under Publius Scipio, the son of the man he had defeated sixteen years earlier, was threatening the city.

At Zama, in 202 B.C., Scipio completely defeated Hannibal, and once again the Carthaginians had to sue for peace. This time they had to give up all their settlements in Spain and the Mediterranean, and all their warships except ten triremes. They had to pay a yearly tribute to Rome and to promise not to wage war without her consent.

Fifty-six years later, after a third short war, Carthage was utterly destroyed. Her inhabitants were killed or enslaved; her treasures were taken to Rome; and the plough was passed over the land, so that no trace of the city was left. Rome was now mistress of the western Mediterranean.

By this time also Rome had extended her sway in the east. Macedonia and Greece had been conquered, and Egypt had become a vassal state. In 133 B.C. the kingdom of Pergamum, in Asia Minor, fell under her rule. From these kingdoms of the Hellenistic world the Romans took Greek statuary to adorn their houses and Greek books to fill their libraries. Greek slaves taught their children, Greek plays were performed in the Roman theatre, and

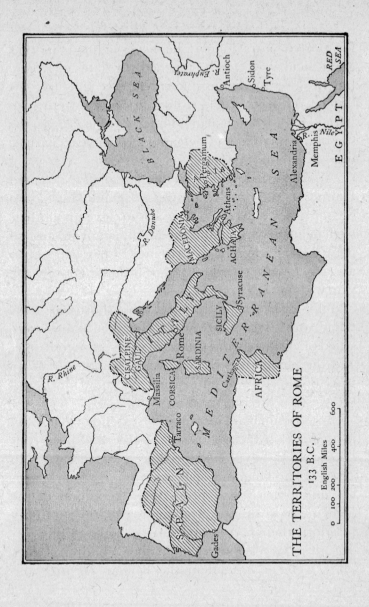

THE TERRITORIES OF ROME

133 B.C.

English Miles

0   100   200   400   600

many Romans forsook their own gods to worship Isis and Apollo. All this brought about great changes in the life of Rome.

The Roman territories outside Italy were governed in a different way from Italy itself. They were divided into provinces. Each province was ruled by a governor, called a proconsul, who was appointed by the Senate. He had soldiers under his command to defend the province. He had to keep order, see that justice was done, and arrange for the collection of the money and produce which every province had to send to Rome as tribute.

At first the proconsuls governed the provinces well, but in time they began to rule less justly, and to allow the tax-collector to take more tribute from the people than was demanded by Rome. So her subjects began to think of Rome as harsh and oppressive, instead of just and considerate, and to be less satisfied with her rule.

CHAPTER XXIX

The troubled days of the Republic

Many troubles befell Rome after the Punic Wars. Rich men became selfish. Poor people became discontented. There was much disorder in Rome. The barbarians attacked the Roman territories.

THE long wars brought about changes in the life of the Roman people. Men became rich through the plunder they gained in war, or through the trade which followed the extension of Roman rule in the Mediterranean. Many of these newly rich Romans used their money selfishly, instead of spending it, like the Greeks and the old-time Romans, for the good of the city. Often they used it to buy up the land of the poorer farmers in Italy, who had fallen into debt while they were serving in the army. Instead of growing corn, they reared sheep on their large estates. They had gangs of slaves, captured in war or bought cheaply in the market-place, to look after the sheep, so that the people of the countryside fell out of work. They left their estates to be managed by bailiffs, while they themselves went to Rome and lived in luxury in the company of wealthy senators, bankers, and big business men.

These were the people who were now of most importance in Rome. They lived on the Palatine Hill in houses adorned with marble columns, mosaic floors, fountains, and statues. They wore expensive clothing and jewellery, and spent a great deal on perfumes and ointments. They gave extravagant dinner-parties and entertainments. When they walked in the city, they were followed by a troop of needy persons who hoped, by flattering them, to obtain gifts and favours from them.

Side by side with this wealthy class were many poor and unemployed. Slaves now did much of the work in the city which had formerly been done by the poorer freemen. Soldiers who had served in the wars came back to Rome, wanting to have an easy life after their hardships. Unemployed farmers drifted into the city to increase the number of workless people, who idled about in the market-places or lounged in the narrow dirty streets between the high wooden tenement-houses in which they lived. They saw their wives and children poorly dressed and badly fed, and they began to ask why some men should have so much money and others so little. Their envy and discontent were increased by the orators who pointed out the extravagances of the rich to the crowds that gathered round them in the Forum. " Who that has the heart of a man, can bear to watch them with their overflowing wealth ? . . . They buy pictures, statuary, plate ; they pull down houses as soon as they are built, and build new ones ; they waste and abuse their wealth. . . . But we have poverty at home and debts in the streets."

There were, however, some thoughtful men in Rome who cared for the welfare of the city and tried to stop the extravagance of the rich, as well as to lessen the hardships of the poor. Cato, a wealthy Roman noble, set an example by his own conduct. He dressed simply, worked with his men on his estate, and taught his children himself, instead of leaving their education to a Greek slave. In the Senate he made speeches against extravagance and evil living. But few listened to Cato ; he was considered old-fashioned.

Tiberius and Gaius Gracchus brought forward laws to restore the land to the farmers ; but the owners banded together against them and prevented them from carrying out their plans. Gaius Gracchus also arranged that corn should be distributed cheaply to the poor. Other men gave free entertainments in the Campus Martius. But this did not help the unemployed to find work ; and, having nothing better to do, they gathered in the streets and taverns, drinking, dicing, and quarrelling. Young men hired bands of idlers to follow them round the streets, robbing and assaulting respectable citizens. When the magistrates tried to pass laws to put an end to their riotous behaviour, they went to the Assembly with their gangsters and terrified the people into

The atrium of a Roman house as it is to-day

The atrium as it was in the second century B.C.

voting against them. Respect for the law, which was one of the best things in Roman life, disappeared, and the only way of keeping order was by means of soldiers quartered in Rome.

Rome was not the only place where there was disorder and discontent. In many of the provinces the people were oppressed by the governors, who taxed them heavily and favoured, in the law courts, the men who made them presents of large sums of money. The sea was unsafe, because pirates abounded, and traders and travellers grumbled loudly. In Italy the countryside was dangerous, owing to the bands of armed men that roamed about, robbing the farmers and murdering those who opposed them. These bands were composed chiefly of slaves, who had run away from the estates on which they worked, because of the cruel way in which they were treated by the overseers. Under a leader called Spartacus they became so strong that the magistrates at Rome had to send an army to subdue them.

Besides all this, Rome was faced with war, both in Italy and on the frontiers. The Roman citizens, grown proud since the Punic Wars, no longer treated the Italians as equals and refused to grant them citizenship as of old. The Italians rebelled against them and were successful enough to force Rome to grant their demands. In Africa war had to be waged against Jugurtha, a Numidian prince, who had cruelly murdered his cousin, who was under Roman protection. The war lasted eight years before Jugurtha was captured and taken to Rome, to be carried in chains in the triumphal procession of Marius, his conqueror.

A greater danger than any of these came from the north, where the barbarians attacked Cisalpine Gaul, which was now a Roman province. The armies that Rome sent to defend the province were defeated several times. Then Marius, who was consul for the first time in 107 B.C., organized and trained an army of paid soldiers, and defeated the barbarians in two great battles. The danger was so great that Marius was elected consul six times in succession. Thus a rule of the Roman state was broken. This had some bad consequences, for it encouraged other men to break the laws for their own advantage, and lessened the respect of the Roman people for the laws concerning their government.

Much of this trouble was due to the fact that the management of the state by the Senate and magistrates was no longer suitable for Rome. A government that can rule a small city is not always the best for a great empire, such as Rome had become. For a democracy to succeed, people must be unselfish, thinking first of the good of the state. In Rome, at this time, there were too many people who thought only of themselves, and cared little for the welfare of the citizens as a whole or for the happiness of the people under Roman rule.

CHAPTER XXX

A great Roman

Julius Caesar added Gaul to the Roman dominions. He tried to put an end to the troubles in Rome. He was murdered because people thought he wished to be king.

JULIUS CAESAR became one of the leading men in Rome about 70 B.C. Though he belonged to a patrician family, he sought to gain the favour of the people; for in Rome now no one could obtain power without popular support. He spent large sums on public games, entertained people of all classes in his house, and was always ready to listen to men's grievances and to promise them help. He joined forces with Crassus, one of the wealthiest men in Rome, and with Pompey, who had gained great popularity by waging a successful war against Mithridates, king of Pontus, and adding four new provinces in Asia to the empire. Aided by these two, he gained the consulship in 59 B.C. After his year of office, he obtained the proconsulship of Gaul, which now extended beyond the Alps into the lower valley of the Rhone. This gave him command of an army which he could use, if necessary, to enforce his will.

The Romans never had a greater general than Julius Caesar. His men would follow him anywhere, for they knew that, if a battle could be won, Caesar would win it. Though he often suffered from a serious illness, he never spared himself. He shared the hardships of his men, and was always in the field to lead and encourage them. "He often alone rallied a wavering line, held up the fugitives, sent men back to the ranks, and turned others towards the enemy, grasping them by the throat, though sometimes he had to deal with men in such a panic that one standard-bearer, thus halted, swung a spear at him, and another abandoned the standard to his clutching hand." Even when he was travelling in his litter, he was at work, dictating letters to his two secretaries or composing chapters of his book, *Concerning the Gallic Wars*, which all school-boys who learn Latin still translate to-day.

During the nine years of his proconsulship, Caesar fought many campaigns against the barbarians beyond the borders of his province. The brave Gallic chieftains were not easily subdued ; but when their leader, Vercingetorix, was defeated and sent prisoner to Rome to be led in chains in his conqueror's triumph, they gave up the struggle, and the whole of Gaul became Roman territory. During these wars Caesar made two expeditions to Britain, exacting tribute from the British chieftains. In his book he describes the island and its people. It is

Caesar who says that the Britons dyed themselves with woad, " which gives them a blue colour and makes them look more terrifying in battle ".

Besides conquering Gaul, Caesar organized it as a Roman province. He allowed the tribes to keep their own customs, and demanded only a small tribute. Many chieftains became Roman citizens.

Captive Gauls in Caesar's triumph

Though he could be cruel on occasions, his rule was, on the whole, just and merciful, and through his work Gaul became one of the most loyal of the Roman provinces.

In 49 B.C. Caesar set out for Rome with his army. The Senate ordered him to disband it. Unless he was prepared to break the law, he must obey the order ; for no general was allowed to bring his army over the river Rubicon, which marked the old boundary between Italy and Cisalpine Gaul, without the Senate's permission. On the river bank Caesar thought for a long time. Then he turned to his soldiers saying, " The die is cast ", which means, " I have made my choice ". He crossed the river and marched on Rome. We still use the phrase " crossing the Rubicon", when we mean that somebody has made a decision which will have serious consequences.

Pompey, who was now working with the Senate against his old friend, went to the East to raise an army ; for there were no soldiers in Rome to equal Caesar's well-trained troops. Caesar followed him and defeated him at Pharsalia in Thessaly. Pompey fled to Egypt, where he was killed, and Caesar, after restoring order in Africa and Asia, returned to Rome.

In their fear of civil war, the Roman people had made Caesar dictator. This was an office which gave him complete power, for a dictator was not bound by the laws. He used his power to try to bring about reforms in Rome and Italy. He founded colonies to which unemployed citizens and discharged soldiers might emigrate, and made new laws for the distribution of corn so that only those in real need obtained it free. Men who would help him in his work were made senators, and the Roman citizenship was granted to the inhabitants of Cisalpine Gaul, so that every free-born Italian was now a Roman citizen. One of the reforms which lasted for many centuries was his improvement of the calendar. The Julian calendar was used in our own country until about two hundred years ago.

Caesar formed plans to beautify Rome and make it a centre of learning, to drain marshes in Italy, and to build roads and canals in the provinces. But, like Alexander the Great, he did not live long enough to carry out his ideas. Though he was trying to rule wisely, he had many enemies. Some people did not like his rule, because they could no longer do just as they pleased. Others believed that he intended to make himself king, even though he refused the title when it was offered him. Though nearly four hundred years had passed since the time of Tarquin the Proud, the Romans still feared and hated the idea of kingship. So in 44 B.C. a number of men plotted to kill Caesar. Their leader was Marcus Brutus, to whom Caesar had shown great kindness. Shakespeare, in his play of *Julius Caesar*, shows how Brutus really believed he was doing a good thing for the state. Brutus says he killed Caesar because he loved Rome : " Had you rather that Caesar were living and die all slaves ; than that Caesar were dead to live all free men ? As Caesar loved me, I weep for him ; as he was fortunate, I rejoice for him ; as he was valiant, I honour him ; but as he was ambitious, I slew him."

Other men saw more truly than Brutus that the murder of Caesar was a disaster for Rome. Rome needed the rule of a single man, who would try to govern for the good of the state as a whole, and would make everybody, rich and poor alike, obey the law. Caesar, even though he was ambitious for power, loved his country and truly wanted to serve her. Fifteen years of warfare and disorder followed his death. Octavian, his great-nephew, and Mark Antony, his friend, set out to avenge his murder. But when they had done this, they quarrelled with one another. The warfare between them went on until 31 B.C., when Antony and his wife, Cleopatra, the beautiful and ambitious queen of Egypt, were defeated at Actium. Two years later Octavian returned to Rome, and the gates of the temple of Janus, which always stood open when Rome was at war, were closed. They had not been closed for two hundred years.

CHAPTER XXXI

Caesar Augustus

Caesar Augustus restored order in Rome. He ruled the Roman world well and kept it at peace. He was the first Roman emperor.

> Roman, be thine
> To sway the world with Empire. These shall be
> Thine arts, to govern with the rule of Peace,
> To spare the weak and subjugate the proud.

VIRGIL wrote these words in the time of Caesar Augustus. This was the name the Romans gave to Octavian, when he became ruler of the Empire. They show how men looked upon Rome as a power that should rule justly and keep peace in the world. It was through the work of Augustus that she was able to do this for more than two hundred years.

Augustus did not, like Julius Caesar, add wide lands to the Empire. He tried to subdue the wild German tribes who lived between the Rhine and the Elbe, and for a short time they were under Roman rule. Then they rose in rebellion, and destroyed a Roman army in a fierce battle. After this, Augustus made no further attempt to rule them, but protected the frontier by placing the legions along it. In some

places on the Rhine, the remains of the legionary
camps can still be seen. They were surrounded by a
ditch and a strong wall, inside which, built in neat
squares, were barracks and storehouses, the soldiers'
forum and the general's quarters. There was also a
temple for the worship of Augustus ; for the emperor
was commander-in-chief of the army, and his worship was part of the military discipline in every camp.
Most of the legions were stationed in camps of this
kind on one or other of the frontiers, for Augustus
did not want the people within the Empire to think
of him as ruling by force. He wanted them to look
upon him as the man they had chosen to govern because of his wisdom and care for their welfare.

Under the rule of Augustus the provinces were
well governed. Honest and industrious governors
were appointed, and the emperor watched and advised them. In most provinces the people had some
share in their own government. They were allowed
to elect the magistrates for their city and their district, as people elect town and county councils to-
day. In the law courts rich men could no longer
bribe the judges to give verdicts in their favour ; for
the emperor was careful to see that poor men as well
as rich were judged fairly. People no longer had to
pay such heavy taxes as in the old days. The governors built baths and theatres in their cities, distributed corn to the poor, and organized games and
other amusements. It was part of their work to look

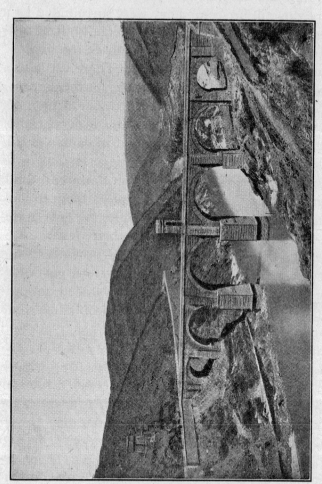

" This bridge great Lacer built with wondrous art "

after the roads and bridges in the province, and to build aqueducts to bring plenty of water to the towns. One of the aqueducts built in the time of Augustus can still be seen near the town of Nîmes in France.

Augustus was the first Roman emperor, but he was not called by this name in Rome. The Latin word, *imperator*, from which comes our word emperor, meant the leader of the army, and was only used by the legions. Instead, he had the title of *princeps*, that is, the first man in the state. The form of government in the city remained the same as in republican times. The consuls, praetors, quaestors and aediles continued their work ; the Senate met regularly to direct affairs ; and the Assembly was summoned to elect the magistrates and to pass the laws. But in spite of this, Augustus was the real ruler, for the magistrates and the Senate acted on his advice, and the people trusted him.

Augustus tried to restore order and good government in Rome, as well as in the provinces. He set an example by living simply, working hard, and attending at the worship of the old Roman gods in their temples. In his palace on the Palatine Hill, he gathered round him men who lived quietly and simply like himself, and poets such as Horace and Virgil, whose poem, the *Aeneid*, tells the story of how Rome became a great city. He made Rome more beautiful by adding to its buildings, and encouraged rich men, like his friends Agrippa and

Maecenas, to spend their money in the same way. He said himself that he found Rome a city of brick and left it a city of marble. Though he was not altogether successful in making people give up their idle and luxurious lives, or in finding work for all the unemployed, he made Rome a much more orderly and prosperous city than it was when he began to rule.

During the two centuries that followed the death of Augustus in A.D. 14, the Roman Empire increased in size and splendour. In 43 the Emperor Claudius began the conquest of Britain, which became a peaceful and prosperous province under the wise rule of Agricola. Trajan, who became emperor in 98, subjected the people of Dacia, a district on the Danube frontier, and began to build a protective wall between the upper courses of the Rhine and the Danube, like that which his successor, Hadrian, built in Britain. Within the Empire the Roman peace made the roads safe for travel and kept the seas free from pirates. Roman customs and the Latin tongue spread among the barbarian tribes. The grant of Roman citizenship to every inhabitant of the Empire, by the Emperor Caracalla, extended Roman law throughout the provinces. The image of the emperor in every city reminded people that they were all under the same rule. So they began to think of themselves as members of the Roman state rather than as Gauls and Africans and Greeks, and to look to Rome as their mother city. Even when, in the fifth

century, Rome's power waned, men still believed
in her greatness ; and Rutilius, a native of Gaul,
praised her in these words :

You brought the nations one great fatherland,
you raised the savage with your taming hand,
broke him, but gave him laws to be his aid.
A City of the scattered Earth you made.

. . . . . .

The Roman pilgrims throng from every side.
Freely the burden of your peace they bear.
The moving stars, eternal, wakeful-eyed,
have seen your empire matchless anywhere.
The furthest East has felt you conquering ;
Assyrians and Medes have knelt in awe ;
on Parthian lord and Macedonian king
you've brought through varying fates one reign
of law.

CHAPTER XXXII

How the Roman world became Christian

Jesus Christ was born in the time of Augustus. His teaching spread through the Roman world. Some emperors persecuted the Christians. Constantine was the first Christian emperor.

" AND it came to pass in those days that there went out a decree from Caesar Augustus that all the world should be taxed." Because of this decree, Joseph and Mary went up to Bethlehem, where Jesus Christ was born.

At this time there were many different kinds of religion in the Roman Empire. Augustus wished people to follow his example and worship the Roman gods, for whom temples were built in the cities of the Empire. He also instituted another form of worship, that of Rome and Augustus. Throughout the Empire altars were set up, to which people came to offer incense before the image of the emperor. Augustus thought this worship important, because it helped people to feel that they were all under the rule of Rome and the emperor, no matter to what race they belonged. But this religion did not make people live good lives, and the old religion of Rome, though it taught men to be honest and sober and to do their duty, did not offer them any help when they were in trouble, or answer their questions about whether there was any other world beyond that in which they lived. So many people turned to other religions, which they thought would help them, though, to avoid punishment, they obeyed the emperor and worshipped in public at the altar of Rome and Augustus.

Some people worshipped Cybele, the mother-goddess of Asia, and others worshipped Isis, the Egyptian goddess. Both these were worshipped with ceremonies which the people themselves did not understand, but which made them feel that the goddesses were more powerful than human beings, and would help them if they obeyed their commands. A god who was worshipped specially by soldiers was Mithras, the Persian god of light. The sacrifice of a bull was the chief feature of his worship, and men believed that he would help them in their fight against evil, and give them courage and endurance. The people of the provinces kept the religion which they had followed before they became subjects of Rome. The Greeks still worshipped the gods of Olympus, and the Jews still held their services in the synagogues and went up to the Temple at Jerusalem.

Other people turned to the wisdom of the Greeks for help. Some followed the teachings of Zeno, who in the third century B.C. had taught in the Stoa, the

" Many roads Thou hast fashioned : all of them lead to the Light "

To the divine Augustus

painted porch in the Agora at Athens. From this his followers were called Stoics. There were many Stoics in imperial Rome. One of the most famous, Epictetus, was born a slave ; another was the Emperor Marcus Aurelius. The Stoics believed that a man should spend his life doing his duty, whether he were a slave or an emperor. He should suffer pain and misfortune calmly, and not be too anxious for happiness and prosperity. Epictetus said life was a play : " Remember that you are an actor in a play . . . your business is to act the character that is given you and act it well ". This belief, though it helped men to live good lives, did not make them sympathetic with others, nor lead them to try to relieve poverty and suffering.

Another teacher, Epicurus, said that people should seek happiness, which would be found by living a good life. Epicurus himself showed that his teaching would make a man kind and considerate for others, but his followers often took it to mean that everyone must seek what he wanted to make his own life pleasant, without thinking of others. So Epicureanism, like Stoicism, did not, in the end, help to make people love their neighbours as themselves. And none of these beliefs gave people any idea of a God who was both just and merciful.

It was Christ's teaching that supplied this need in the Roman world. The book of the Acts of the Apostles tells how His gospel was spread through

Asia Minor and Greece, and how little groups of
Christians grew up in many cities. When St. Paul
reached Rome in A.D. 61, he found some followers of
Christ already there ; and during the years that he
lived in the city, they grew in numbers. At first no
notice was taken of them by the magistrates, who
looked upon Christi-
anity as only one more
of the religions in
Rome. But when the
Christians refused to
worship at the altar
of Augustus, they were
punished for disobedi-
ence to the law. They
also fell into disfavour
because they met to-
gether in private for
services. The emperors
refused to allow secret

A sign used by Christians

meetings of any kind, for they thought the people
might use them to plot against their power. Many
people disliked them also because their teaching,
especially about the treatment of slaves, was contrary
to the usual practice among the Romans, and because they condemned the cruelty shown in the
games and gladiatorial shows. In the reign of Nero
persecution began. Tradition says it was then that
St. Paul was put to death. Every bad thing that

happened was put down to the Christians ; among
other things, they were charged with starting the fire
that destroyed a large part of the city in A.D. 64.
Some were crucified, others were tortured and
burned, and many were thrown to the lions in the
Colosseum.

For more than two hundred years after this the
Christians were always in danger of persecution.
Under some emperors, such as Domitian and Dio-
cletián, it was very severe. Other emperors, though
they ordered the punishment of the Christians because they refused to obey the law, did not hunt
them out and punish them simply for their beliefs ;
for they saw that their lives were better than those
of many other people. We know from a letter which
Trajan wrote to Pliny, his governor in Bithynia, what
was his practice with regard to Christians. He said,
" Do not go out of your way to look for these people.
If they are brought before you and proved guilty,
they must be punished—with this reservation, that if
anyone says he is not a Christian, and proves the
truth of his words by praying to our gods, then he is
to be pardoned, whatever be his past record."

In spite of persecution, the Christians increased
greatly in numbers, for their teaching about God and
the life after death was what many people were seeking. The goodness of their daily lives, their care for
the sick and the poor, and the courage with which
they endured martyrdom impressed people greatly.

I

Q

At last there came an emperor, Constantine, who, though he was not actually baptized till the end of his life, probably believed in the Christian teaching. He tells the story of how, when he was preparing for a battle against a rival emperor, " about noon, when the day was already beginning to decline, he saw with his own eyes the trophy of a cross of light in the heavens, above the sun, bearing the inscription, *In this sign thou shalt conquer* ". He won the battle, and in A.D. 313 he issued an edict which gave the followers of any religion freedom to worship as they thought right. A later emperor, Theodosius, went still farther and said that all the people in the Empire must be Christians. In this way Christianity took the place of the old religions of Greece and Rome, and the bishops and priests of the Christian Church taught the gospel of Christ throughout the Roman world.

CHAPTER XXXIII

Imperial Rome

Imperial Rome was a magnificent city. There was much wealth and luxury, but also much unemployment. The emperor had many servants who kept good order in the city.

A CITIZEN of one of the provinces, visiting Rome in A.D. 220, would be amazed at its magnificence. He would stroll through new forums, each with its basilica and temple, its shops and offices, rivalling the old Forum in the splendour of marble colonnades and bronze statuary. He would worship in the temple of the Divine Julius, whom Augustus had taught the people to regard as a god. He would gaze in awe at the tall column of Trajan, carved with pictures of his wars in Dacia, and linger in his spacious libraries, with their rows of parchment and papyrus rolls, containing the works of Greek and Latin writers. He would mount the Sacred Way to the triumphal arch of Titus, with its sculptured pictures of his prowess against the rebellious Jews in A.D. 70. Beyond it he would see one of the finest of Rome's public buildings, the temple of Venus and Roma, and the Colosseum, the immense amphi-

233

theatre where gladiators, drawn from all nations,
fought one another to the death to amuse the Roman
populace. Gazing at its solidity and strength, he
would perhaps recall the prophecy concerning it :

> While stands the Colosseum, Rome shall stand ;
> When falls the Colosseum, Rome shall fall ;
> And when Rome falls, the world.

The provincial might go next to the Circus Maxi-
mus, still the arena for the chariot races and the
sports lavishly provided by the emperors. From there
he could go on to the Campus Martius, the parade
ground of the republican legions. Here he would see
the Altar of Peace, decreed by the Senate to commemorate the deeds of Augustus ; from the reliefs
sculptured on the marble walls of its courtyard, he
could learn many things about the customs of Rome
two hundred years ago. He could rest in one of the
porticoes in the beautiful public gardens surrounding
it ; then he could visit the mausoleum of Augustus
and the Pantheon, a stately temple for the images of
the supreme gods. Here he would see the name of its
builder, Agrippa, carved upon the lintel of the Greek
portico, and marvel at the fine concrete dome with
which Hadrian had crowned the massive walls of the
temple itself. Near the theatre of Pompey, the first
stone theatre in Rome, he would see the theatre of
Marcellus, and not far off, the baths of Agrippa. Once
a wide open space, the Campus Martius had been

The triumphal arch of Titus

covered with fine buildings and laid out with gardens, fountains and statuary by successive emperors, to commemorate themselves and to add to the splendour of the capital.

A visitor to imperial Rome would not be content with sight-seeing. He would want to learn something about Roman life as well. If he were a man of wealth and influence in his own city, he would bring letters of introduction to important people in Rome. Through the good offices of an imperial official, he might gain entry to the palace of the Caesars. At the gateway he would have to pass the famous praetorian guards, the only soldiers who were stationed in Rome. Without guidance he would lose himself in the vast palace, with its porches and its vestibules, its corridors, anterooms, libraries, and marble halls. If he were fortunate enough to be received in audience by the emperor, he would marvel at the luxury of his private apartments, his silken robes and scented hair, and the number of his slaves and attendants.

The wealthy provincial would be a frequent visitor at the big houses in Rome. He would attend the morning reception of the great man, and watch him dispense his favours among the crowd gathered around him, giving a present to one, promising an office to another, laughing graciously at the witty story of a third. He would have many invitations to dinner-parties, sometimes in the house of a wealthy profiteer, who gave his guests rich food and much

wine, and talked principally about the way in which
he had made his money, sometimes in the home of a
dignified Roman noble, where the chief enjoyment

Praetorian guards

was the talk about books and learning, the arguments
and the amusing stories that filled the intervals between the courses.

During his stay he would go frequently to the
baths of Caracalla, where everybody of importance
in Rome was to be seen. Here, before bathing, he

could exercise in the gymnasium; afterwards he could take a light meal in the restaurant, read in the library, or amuse himself in one of the spacious marble halls. He might spend a few days at the seaside villa of one of his acquaintances, travelling with his host in a litter hung with embroidered curtains and carried by burly slaves. In the airy sunny rooms he would be refreshed after the stuffy heat of Rome, and spend pleasant hours admiring the gardens, swimming in the bathing-pool, and talking over the questions of the day with other guests.

A magistrate or a business man would want to see how the government and the business of Rome were carried on. He might go to the harbour of Ostia, laid out with new quays and warehouses by the Emperor Claudius, visit some of the factories of Rome, and notice the high prices of food and clothing compared with those of his own city. He might listen to a debate in the Senate, and find out how the aediles kept order in the streets and taverns, organized the public games, and distributed the corn dole. He would be interested in the aqueducts that brought water from the hills around Rome to supply the public fountains and the large private houses. He would inspect the fire brigade and visit the temple of Aesculapius, where the sick poor could obtain free treatment from the priests. He would find the schools of Rome were not very different from those of his own city. He would see arithmetic, reading, and writing (the self-

A schoolboy's Greek exercise

same letters that we use in print to-day) being taught
in the schools for younger boys. In the grammar
schools he would find their elder brothers studying
Greek and the poems of Homer, as well as the works
of the great Roman writers. Roman schoolboys read
Virgil and Horace as British schoolboys read Shake-

speare and Wordsworth, and studied the speeches of Cicero, in order that they might learn how to speak well in public themselves.

The crowded streets of Rome were full of interest for the visitor. Processions paraded the streets, a bride in her white dress and flame-coloured veil being escorted to her new home, priests celebrating the festival of their god, the consul attended by his lictors, an imperial officer escorted by praetorian guards. Street booths lined the poorer thoroughfares; pedlars hawked gaudy trinkets, quack medicines, and cheap wares of every kind; beggars lounged at the street corners; women chattered beside the fountains. Roman ladies, their faces painted and their hair extravagantly dressed, paraded the streets, attended by their slaves; and countrymen, in leather tunics and sandals stuffed with straw, drove their heavy wooden carts over the stone paving with an ear-splitting clatter. Slaves were to be found everywhere. After the gaiety of Roman life, a visitor might think life in his own city rather dull. But he might also think that, in some ways, it was better. Drinking and gambling and vulgar show were too common in Rome; everywhere was noise and bustle, and there were too many imperial spies about for a man to be altogether comfortable.

CHAPTER XXXIV

An Italian city

Pompeii was a little copy of Rome. It had a forum and temples, baths and theatres, and many large houses. The city was destroyed by an eruption of Mount Vesuvius.

IN November, A.D. 79, the town of Pompeii, at the foot of Mount Vesuvius, was a gay happy place. In December it was a desolate heap of cinders and ashes, rained down upon it during the eruption of the volcano above it. So it remained for seventeen hundred years. Then excavators began to dig out the city, and to-day there can be seen at Pompeii the almost complete plan of an Italian town.

In form Pompeii was, like other Italian and provincial towns, a small copy of Rome. Except on the side towards the sea, it was surrounded by a wall, with towers and gates at intervals. In the middle of the city was the forum, its walls and colonnades decorated, not with marble, but with patterns and pictures painted in gay colours. Around the forum were the public buildings of the city; the council-house and the magistrates' offices, the basilica where the law courts were held, the temples of Jupiter and of Apollo, and

the shrine of Rome and Augustus. There also were
the two chief markets of the town, the meat market

and the cloth exchange. As in Rome,
the forum was the centre of civic life,
thronged with magistrates, lawyers,
orators, and business men, as well as
country folk and slaves, beggars and
idlers.

From the forum straight streets ran
to the different gates of the city. The
Marine Parade led to the harbour,
where the fishing fleet and the private
yachts of rich residents were moored.
Greek and other foreign coasting vessels
were often to be seen in the harbour.
The streets were paved with large blocks of lava,
worn into deep ruts by the constant passage of lum-
bering wooden carts,
bringing country
produce to the Pom-
peian markets. A
raised pavement on
either side and step-
ping-stones at corners
were provided by the
city authorities, so

that the elegant visitors who came to the little
town might not soil their soft leather shoes and
embroidered sandals in the muddy street.

Excavations have brought to light many large houses in the fashionable quarter of the city. Some of these were probably apartment houses for visitors ; others the homes of rich Pompeian citizens or of Roman nobles, many of whom had villas in Pompeii. They were similar in plan to a Roman house. The *atrium*, with its mosaic floor and painted walls, its bronze statuettes and carved furniture, was as elegant, even if not as expensive, as that of a big house on the Palatine Hill. Beyond the large room at the farther end, used by the master of the house as a reception room, was a garden with flower-beds, ponds, fountains and statues. Sometimes this garden was surrounded by a colonnade and living-rooms ; a winter dining-room and a summer dining-room, a sitting-room and a loggia, nurseries and bedrooms. Sometimes it was not enclosed ; then the rooms round the *atrium*, otherwise kept for business purposes and for the household slaves, were used as living-rooms. There were few windows looking out on the street, but some houses had balconies, from which the occupants could watch the busy scene below.

In this quarter also were the important shops of the town. They were built into the walls of the big houses. The Pompeian shopkeeper had but little space to store his goods ; he was fortunate if he had a small room behind the shop, and an even smaller one above. None the less, there was plenty of business done in Pompeii. Silversmiths, jewellers, cutlers, leather-workers, potters, and glass-makers displayed their wares on low open counters, closing their shops at night with wooden shutters. Perfumers tempted the Pompeian ladies with the latest novelties in

In a baker's yard

powder and scent. The delicacies in the cooked-food shops offered housewives an easy way of providing a meal. The dark interiors of the wine-shops were a refuge from the hot glare of the sun, and their owners did a thriving trade. From the bakers' shops came the harsh grinding of the mill, as its stones revolved one upon another, and the fragrant smell of newly baked bread. The business men of Pompeii had little need to grumble about bad trade, for the visitors to the town spent their money freely.

In the poorer quarters of the town were the tanneries and the blacksmiths' shops, the workrooms of the fullers who bleached the fine white wool for the citizens' togas, and the dyers who dyed linen in delicate colours for the dresses of their wives and daughters. Among the dust and smell from these the working people plied their various trades, lounged in the narrow streets, gossiped around the public fountains, and ate and slept in houses or flats of three or four rooms. The bare stucco walls of the tenement houses were drab in comparison with the painted walls of the big villas ; but they provided a useful place for writing public notices and advertisements. Here are some which can still be seen to-day : " Property of Julia Spurenna, daughter of Felix. To let : Baths of Venus (90th), shops, stalls, upper rooms, on a five years' lease, beginning from the 1st of August. Enquiries invited." " Vote for G. Julius Polybius as aedile. He bakes good bread." And scribbled by an idler, " Good luck to the man who'll invite me to a meal ".

Like every other town, Pompeii had its public baths, equipped with a gymnasium and rest-rooms. It had two theatres, and barracks for the gladiators, whose contests took place in the amphitheatre. These spectacles were widely advertised : " The Gladiator

School of the Aedile A. Suettius Certus will give an Exhibition at Pompeii on the last day of May. Hunting Shows and Awnings. All Nero's Spectacles. No stunting." Taverns near by provided refreshment for the patrons of the theatres, and lodgings for the strolling players who came to the town. These players were a noisy, easy-going, and sometimes quarrelsome company. Each actor wanted to play the star part. The boys who took the women's parts annoyed their elders, and went off on excursions to the seashore, when they should have been ready to rehearse. The manager's life was not an easy one. He had to keep everybody in a good temper, deal with emergencies such as the non-arrival of the properties or the death of his best baggage-donkey, and, if the public did not support the show, bear the brunt of the landlord's anger when there was no money to pay his bill.

CHAPTER XXXV

Prosperity and downfall

Trade prospered in the peaceful Roman Empire. Rome was the chief trading city. Roads led from it to the large cities in the provinces. Prosperity ended when the barbarians invaded the Empire. Rome was no longer mistress of the world.

In the reign of Marcus Aurelius the orator Aristides said, " What could be better than the present state of affairs ? Now any man can go whither he pleases with absolute confidence, the harbours of the Empire are full of business, even the mountains are safe for those who journey over them, as the cities are to those who dwell in them."

This security, which was the result of the emperors' strong rule, led to a great increase in the trade of the Roman Empire. In Rome and the provincial cities, rich business men took their place in the upper classes side by side with magistrates, senators, and men of noble birth. Bankers lent money to fit out trading vessels, and to provide large buildings in which slaves turned out goods under the direction of the master or his overseer. Hundreds of slaves were occupied in mining gold, silver, lead, tin, and copper.

Foreign merchants were to be seen in all the ports of the Empire. New shops and offices were opened in the cities, where slaves who had bought their freedom set up in business for themselves. All this brought about a change in the habits of the Roman people. Farmers were still to be found in Italy and in the provinces, and poets praised the simplicity of country life.

> I praise the man who draws his children round,
> and, aging in his cottage, laughs at care.
> He guides the sheep, his son the lambs, by day.
> His wife prepares the water for his bath.

But more and more people depended upon industry and commerce for their living. The improvement of trade became an important part of the work of the emperor's servants and of the provincial governors.

Rome was the centre of what is called to-day big business. Roads like the Appian Way, which had been made in republican times, all started from Rome; and the new roads, driven through the provinces by order of the emperors, were linked up with them. The trade routes across the Mediterranean from Spain, Africa, Egypt, and the cities of Asia all led to Ostia or Puteoli. Every province of the Empire helped to supply the needs of the large population of the city. Marble, granite, and timber for buildings, wool, linen and leather for clothing, bronze and iron for household goods, gold, silver, and precious stones for jewellery, these were only a few of the things that found their way to Rome. Corn was imported in large quantities for free distribution to the poor, as well as cattle and fish, wine and oil. Roman merchants traded as far afield as China, to obtain silk for the use of the emperor and his household, and jade for the ornaments of the wealthy Roman ladies. Perfumes from Egypt, purple dye from Tyre, the amber of the Baltic, the oysters of the British coasts, ivory, spices, and pearls from the East, and the syrup of the sugar-cane from India, were among the rarer articles which found a market in Rome. It was no wonder that Aristides called the city " the general workshop of the whole world ".

Rome was not the only centre of business in the Empire. In the provinces also there were trading cities like Lyons, with their wealthy merchants and skilled artisans. The harbours of the Mediterranean, of Spain and Gaul and Britain, were nearly as busy as Ostia. Transport barges plied up and down the rivers, and trains of heavily loaded waggons blocked the roads. The spread of Roman customs led to a demand in the provinces for the luxuries enjoyed in Rome. Provincial traders and craftsmen found a ready market for their wares in their own province, as well as in Rome.

This trading activity had many good results. It gave employment, improved people's ways of living, and increased their knowledge of the world. Merchants often used their wealth for the benefit of

their town, erecting fine buildings, providing public
libraries, and organizing games for their fellow citizens. But it also had some bad results. There were
profiteers in the Roman Empire, and employers
who sweated their workers in order that they might
live in luxury themselves. Many people became so
occupied with money-making that they cared for
little else. Men were judged according to the amount
of money they had, not according to whether they
were educated men and good citizens. v.G

The Emperor Marcus Aurelius died in A.D. 180.
From this time onwards, the peace and prosperity of
the Roman Empire slowly disappeared. Many of
the emperors were cruel and selfish, spending the
money which they exacted from their subjects on
their numerous palaces, their rich clothing, and their
extravagant banquets and amusements. Others were
weak men who were quite unfit for the work of
government, which they now tried to do by themselves, without the help of the senate and magistrates.
Sometimes there were rival emperors, one chosen by
the legions and the other by the praetorian guards
in Rome. Then there was fighting between them,
until one of them was killed. The provinces were
not so well ruled, because the governors, who were
often imperial favourites, neglected their work.
The people suffered from famines and pestilence,
land went out of cultivation, and traders were at
the mercy of the brigands who infested the roads.

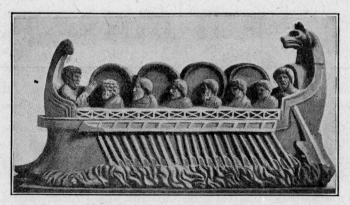

Transporting wine down the Rhine

A banker in a Roman province

The provincials began to murmur at the burden laid upon them. They found it difficult to pay the heavy taxes levied by the emperors. The Italians became more and more unwilling to serve in the legions, and the task of defending the frontiers proved too heavy for the auxiliary forces recruited from the provinces. Since the time of Augustus the barbarians had been held at bay ; now they began once more to invade the Roman territories. During the fifth century Goths and Vandals settled in Southern Gaul, Spain and Africa. Angles, Saxons, and Jutes invaded Britain. The savage Huns swept through the land, burning and destroying, until their leader, Attila, was defeated and killed at Châlons in 451. Rome itself was not spared by the barbarians. Alaric the Goth sacked and burned it in 410 ; forty-five years later it was besieged by the Vandal leader, Genseric ; and in 476 the German, Odoacer, entered the city and deposed the Emperor Romulus Augustulus.

This was the end of Rome as an imperial city, but it was not the end of the Roman Empire. The emperors continued to rule in Constantinople (the ancient city of Byzantium), which had been made into a second capital of the Empire by Constantine the Great. But the territory over which they ruled was only a small part of the empire of Augustus ; the rest was broken up into barbarian kingdoms.

Though Rome had fallen, the Roman civilization did not entirely disappear. Some of the barbarian tribes were Christians, and they spared the Christian churches. In their parishes and dioceses the priests and bishops tried to maintain the order that had been kept by the Roman magistrates, and to teach the barbarians Roman ways. Roman buildings remained to be used again in later days. Some of the roads and bridges that the Romans built are still in use to-day. Roman customs survived in many places. The law of some European countries is founded upon the law of Rome, and the speech of Frenchmen, Spaniards, and Italians springs from the Latin language.

CHAPTER XXXVI

Our legacy from ancient times

Many things we use to-day were invented by the people of the Ancient East. The Greeks gave us beautiful poetry and sculpture. From both Greeks and Romans we have learned how to govern ourselves and other people. The Romans spread the Christian religion.

IN the four thousand years that lie between the rise of the Sumerian cities and the fall of Rome, many changes took place in the world whose centre was the Mediterranean Sea. Since the fall of Rome, nearly fifteen hundred years ago, other changes have taken place in a far wider world. Some people may think that these changes are more important than those of ancient times. They may point to machinery, to modern methods of transport, to newspapers, wireless, and telephones, to discoveries in the world of science and medicine, to the abolition of slavery, the institution of hospitals and old-age pensions, and say that these are the important things in our lives to-day. But if we think a little, we shall see that all these things would not have come about, if the way had not been prepared for them. Moreover, a world which had only these things in them would be an incomplete world. Our heritage from ancient times is still an important part of our lives.

The people of the Ancient East were the inventors of many arts still necessary to us, such as building, agriculture, canal-making, and the manufacture of clothing, furniture, and pottery. They invented also many things which, though not necessary, are still widely used, such as jewellery, paint and powder. Their practice of exchanging goods was the beginning of trade ; their reed boats and donkey caravans were the earliest form of transport. They began painting and sculpture, writing, literature and measurement. They had laws and government, and their kings ruled over wide lands. To the Hebrews, a people of the Ancient East, we owe our belief in one God only. In some of their arts the ancient peoples had not progressed very far. A Sumerian statue often seems to us out of proportion, and the quaint paintings of the Egyptians show that they knew nothing about the laws of perspective. They were ignorant of many things which are now common knowledge, and they had little of the freedom and variety in work and play that we enjoy to-day.

The next steps in progress were made by the Greeks. They learned some things from the earlier civilization of Asia and Egypt. Greek temples are built on the same principle as Egyptian ones. The stiff form and straight lines of early Greek statues show how Greek sculptors were influenced by Egyptian art. The beautiful little carvings on precious stones, in which the Greeks excelled, are like Sumerian and Egyptian seal carvings. In the stories of Homer there are similarities to the story of Gilgamesh ; in mathematics the Greeks learned much from the Egyptians. Greek writing can be traced through the Phoenicians back to cuneiform writing ; wax tablets are only another form of clay tablets ; and papyrus was a common writing material among the Greeks. In trade the Greeks owed much to earlier peoples : weights and measures come down from the earliest traders, the Sumerians ; and the invention of coinage, which helped to increase Greek trade so greatly, took place in Asia Minor.

But though the Greeks owed much to earlier peoples, they still added much themselves. Their poetry and their art are among the most beautiful in the world. In learning they discovered things entirely unknown to the ancients, and introduced a new way of thinking about the world, trying to explain naturally happenings which before had been ascribed simply to the will of the gods. They extended education to include that of the body as well as the mind. To the Greeks we owe the principle of government under which we live to-day, the idea that each man should help in the management of the affairs of his country and his town, and take part in the administration of the law. It is true that the Greeks did not apply this idea completely, for a large part of the population in every city was composed of slaves and foreigners, who had no citizen rights. But even so, they went far beyond the ancient peoples, whose only idea of government was that of an all-powerful ruler.

To the Romans also we owe much. First of all, they preserved and extended the civilization of the Greeks. They also contributed much of their own. As the Romans were above all things a practical people, they added, not so much new ideas as new and improved ways of applying old ideas. They made better roads and bridges than any other people ; they showed that they understood the importance of good water supplies by constructing aqueducts ; they improved the art of building by using concrete as well as brick, stone and timber, and by introducing again vaults and arches in their baths and basilicas and big houses. They made great changes in business methods, trading much farther afield than the Greeks had done, and building up big industries. The beginning of business on a large scale, so familiar to us to-day, is to be found in the Roman Empire. Theyimproved upon many earlier arts, such as glass-making, and introduced new plants and animals into different parts of the Empire. Apple trees and hens were both brought to Britain by the Romans.

The Romans also contributed much to the practice of government. They showed men how to govern wide lands successfully. They taught people to live by the rule of law and to respect the authority of the magistrates, ideas which underlie our conduct as citizens to-day. In the Roman Empire the Christian Church grew up, and it is the teaching of Christianity that guides our daily lives.

" Seafaring and agriculture, fortification, law, weapons, roadmaking, clothing and all else belonging to it, . . . music, painting, and the shaping of cunning statues—all these experience taught to men as they advanced slowly step by step—experience and the adventures of man's tireless mind." These are the words of Lucretius, a Roman writer. He saw how the world he knew had been shaped by the thoughts and deeds of the people who had lived before him. Nearly fifteen hundred years have passed since the fall of Rome ; the story of men's thoughts and deeds during that time links the Roman world with the world of to-day.

INDEX

The following symbols are used to indicate pronunciation :—

ā as in *pay*   ĕ as in *end*   ŏ as in *not*
ă ,, ,, *at*   ī ,, ,, *pine*   ū ,, ,, *use*
à ,, ,, *part*   ĭ ,, ,, *pin*   ŭ ,, ,, *utter*
ē ,, ,, *mete*   ō ,, ,, *note*   th ,, ,, *thought*

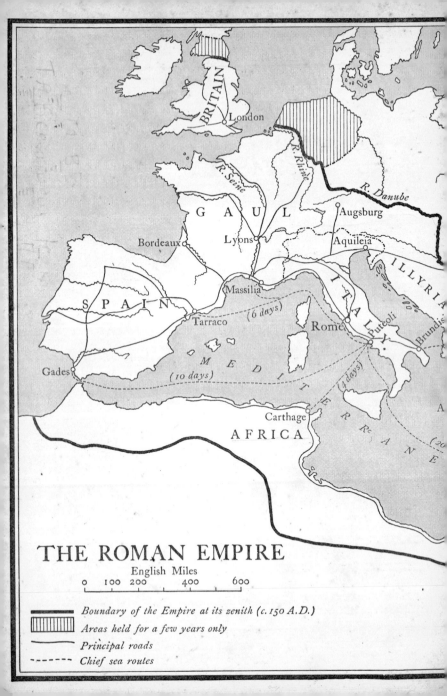

THE ROMAN EMPIRE

English Miles

0   100 200   400   600

━━━━ *Boundary of the Empire at its zenith (c. 150 A.D.)*

▥▥▥ *Areas held for a few years only*

───── *Principal roads*

------- *Chief sea routes*